# WHY HORSES

# WHY HORSES
## poems

*Anita K. Boyle*

MoonPath Press

Copyright © 2020 Anita K. Boyle

All rights reserved. No part of this publication may be reproduced, distributed, or transmitted in any form or by any means whatsoever without written permission from the publisher, except in the case of brief excerpts for critical reviews and articles. All inquiries should be addressed to MoonPath Press.

Poetry
ISBN 978-1-936657-50-6

Cover art "Sunset Ride" copyright © 2020 by Anita K. Boyle
Author photo copyright © 2020 by Abram Olson

Book design by Tonya Namura using Fairplex Narrow OT
MoonPath Press is dedicated to publishing the finest poets living in the U.S. Pacific Northwest.

MoonPath Press
PO Box 445
Tillamook, OR 97141
MoonPathPress@gmail.com

http://MoonPathPress.

# Acknowledgements

"About Writing Political Poetry," *Take a Stand, Art Against Hate: A Raven Chronicles Anthology*, 2020

"Song of the Orca," *For Love of Orcas: An Anthology*, Wandering Aengus Press, 2019

"The Mole", "First Primer," *Footbridge Above the Falls* anthology, Rose Alley Press, 2019

"Janitor of the Labyrinth," "The Green Pear," *Bracken Magazine*, 2018

"Ode to the Beer-Colored Moon," *Last Call: The Anthology of Beer, Wine & Spirits Poetry*, World Enough Writers, 2018

"As Wild Geese Gather," *WA 129*, Sage Hill Press, 2017

"A Lesson Learned," *The 2017 Poetry Marathon Anthology*, Authors Publish Press, 2017

"Walk Away Wisely," *Adventures NW*, 2016

"Moody Interruptions on a Nurse Log," "A Comparison With or Without an Eagle," "Will of the Children," "My Life," *Clover Literary Rag* Various publication dates

*The Drenched: A Creation Myth for the Pacific Northwest*, Egress Studio Press, 2014

"Day of Thrush Songs," *Northwind Poets Anthology*, 2013

"An Abridged Year, Condensed," "Bezoar for My Youth," *Poets on Assignment: Variations on a Prompt*, SpeakEasy 7 anthology, 2012

"Time With Cats," *Crab Creek Review*

"Night Air," *Bamboo Equals Loon*, 2001

*with reverence for
Flicka and Moby*

# Table of Contents

## *Landscape of the Moment*
- 5   Landscape of the Moment
- 7   The Octopus' Gaze
- 9   The Song of the Orca
- 12   About Gratitude
- 13   Neap Tide Rising
- 14   Arguing with Rumi
- 15   The New Poem
- 16   Bearing Notes
- 18   Homage to Josef Albers
- 19   Mona's Boredom
- 21   The Metaphysics of Figure & Ground
- 23   Janitor of the Labyrinth
- 25   The Door
- 26   A Comparison With or Without an Eagle
- 27   Will of the Children
- 28   This is the Way It Doesn't Work
- 31   Lines
- 32   Ode to the Beer-Colored Moon
- 35   Can You Hear Me?
- 37   Ode to the River Willow
- 39   Abandoning Spring
- 40   In the Beginning
- 41   I Thought I Saw Your Underwear
- 43   The Lawn Mower
- 44   Freeze Frame
- 45   Ode to the Cherry Tomato
- 46   Exactly Verbatim, an Unsung Opera: The Summary
- 48   Cascadia: a Love Song in Seven Parts
- 52   Unraveling the Gossamer Silk of Thought

## *Letter for the Day After Tomorrow*
- 55   Letter for the Day After Tomorrow
- 56   Walk Away Wisely

| | |
|---|---|
| 58 | The Weather of Transition |
| 60 | First Darkness |
| 62 | Spotting an Owl in a New-Mown Field |
| 63 | The Mole |
| 64 | Unless It Rains |
| 66 | Reckless Grace |
| 68 | The Green Pear |
| 69 | A Day of Thrush Songs |
| 71 | The Tardy Garden of Late June |
| 73 | What the Buzz is All About |
| 74 | The Ant Hill Beside the Sweet Peas |
| 77 | The Pond Takes an Afternoon Nap |
| 78 | The River Decides to Flood |
| 80 | Bezoar of Spring |
| 82 | As Spring Marches Louder |
| 84 | Hummingbird Renditions |
| 86 | Early One Morning |
| 87 | Moody Interruptions on a Nurse Log |
| 91 | The Glow of Petals |
| 92 | The Drenched: A Creation Myth for the Pacific Northwest |
| 96 | Frogs of the Evening |
| 97 | The Tenor |
| 98 | First Frost |
| 99 | Dear Elephant |
| 100 | About Writing Political Poetry |
| 102 | Dear Gerald Stern |
| 104 | Song of the Liar |
| 106 | Lost Shadow |
| 107 | An Abridged Year, Condensed |
| 109 | Five Fields |
| 110 | Mosquitoes |
| 112 | If You Must Crow, Unsew Your Mouth, Open Wide, and Let the Flies Begin |
| 115 | Existential Pastoral |
| 117 | Earnestly Banished |

118 Sitting Like Clowns
119 Meat and Potatoes
120 What Tasted Bad Then and Still Does Today

### *The Importance of Average Miracles*
125 The Importance of Average Miracles
128 The Egg is a Damsel
129 Buttercups
130 Why Roosters Are Odious
131 Why a Chicken Lays an Egg
133 When a One-Eyed Sphinx Moth Lays an Egg
134 Pastoral: Late August, Mid-Morning
135 The Impact of Beauty
137 The Bearer of Light and Dark
139 Questioning the Immortality of Horses
141 Like Wings
142 The Orchard
144 The Forceps Baby
145 Summary of Our Childhood
147 The Line-Up
148 Ode to My Unpresent Tonsils
150 When Thorns of the Hawthorn Pierce the Soul
152 Chewing Gum, a Pity
154 Growing Pains
156 An Early Primer
158 Once I had a Dad
160 In Another Life
162 Ode to the Sliver in My Left-Hand's Middle Finger
165 Last Year's Lost & Found
167 A Lesson Learned
168 Learning to Dance
169 Bezoar for My Youth
171 Enunciation of the Minced Oath
173 The Scope
175 The Phone Rang Just Before Breakfast
177 Wet Heads

| | |
|---|---|
| 180 | One Morning, and the Window |
| 182 | Without the Sun |
| 183 | The Homestead |
| 184 | A Ride Through the Park |
| 186 | Instead of a Dog |
| 188 | History Lesson in Four Parts |
| 191 | There Was a Time |
| 193 | Morphine |
| 196 | Grocery Shopping with Mom |
| 199 | Dark Chocolate and Almonds |
| 201 | Morning World |
| 202 | Driving Down Sunset |
| 203 | A Detail |
| 204 | Under Direwood |
| 205 | Right Angles |
| 207 | The Weather of Night Horses |
| 208 | There Are Horses in Heaven |
| 209 | The Redolent Wings of Dawn |
| 211 | Time with Cats |
| 213 | On Breaking My Leg |
| 214 | Though Strange, Though Enough |
| 215 | Biking Up the Driveway and Back |
| 216 | My Life |
| 217 | Night Air |
| 218 | View from the Upstairs Studio Window |
| 219 | Cabin on Lummi Island |
| 220 | As Wild Geese Gather |
| 221 | Vehicle of the Muse |
| 222 | Why Horses |
| | |
| 223 | Gratitude |
| 225 | About the Author |

# WHY HORSES

*Landscape of the Moment*

## Landscape of the Moment

The door is ajar. The Pacific Ocean
is growling, a wolf in the underbrush.
The unfriendly tide froths
at the doorstep, rabid.

In the salty grit of the sea,
a bellowing strip of gray-green
shows up. The swindling reek
of saline tags along. The scent

of sunlight leaks like oil
from the broken sand dollar.
The memory of flatness resides
along the brutal shoreline.

With this view, even Basho
would be silent for a time.
The door has creaked wide open.
The sun is a juicy peach

behind the ominous bruise of the clouds.
If the wind weren't howling so hard,
the fierce waves would ebb.
Dog-gone it, this

is what beauty is about.
And who gives a dang?
Once the dog fetches the stick,
the tide will turn. Once the old mare

appears on the sand, the distraction
begins. The silky darkness of stars
flutters across the door jamb
and enters the room. A festering wave

of helplessness sometimes overwhelms,
a jug of ice, sweating on the railing. The ocean
eventually flattens, becomes smooth as a paper
set on a table. We have to trust this is so.

## The Octopus' Gaze

She sees the anemone.
Stubby arms thrash about
in search of the tiniest crumb.
Arms now sunlit and graceful,
moving like a long, long line of dancers
rehearsing at the barre.

She sees the urchin.
The snail.
The star.

The miniature lobster
we call the spot prawn.
It will keep its head a while
longer, though it is already
a pink as pretty
as cooked shrimp.

She sees the rockfish.
The limpet.
The chiton.

The sea cucumber
pickling itself in the brine
of the ocean: a lewd creature
who moves by ooze
across everything in sight,
its bones shaped like wooden-spoked
wheels to go, and anchors to hold fast.

She sees the long fronds,
the delicate curls of her legs,
an abacus of tentacles.

She cannot see
her own beautiful eyes.
The horizon line of her pupil,
as she settles docile as a cow
into the rocks. The turbulence
of her craggy Kodachrome skin
calming from storm to the flat
line of the turning tide.

## The Song of the Orca

A long time ago,
back when the oceans
were silent, and feathers of
fragments drifted wave to current,
whirl to eddy, and dribbled
slow into the cracks of the sand.
Back when darkness was the light,
and the light, therefore, was darkness.
Back even further, when the heat
of the sun was the surface of the earth,
and the earth having no surface
worth mentioning, was ashamed.

That small particle became
the world's first sound. "Which one?"
you might ask, "Which particle?" No matter.
There was a sound just the same.
And where it came from is of no concern
today, nor when it was made.

But from that sound came
the round ball, the pull of gravity, the small
bend of the horizon to the eye, the single nostril
of the whale we call the orca. This was more
than the earth could take back then,

and so this noise, the one particle of sound,
was put on hold. Kept precious and separate
from all the particles that floated
across the ocean. Other fractures splintered.
Became a sludge, a muck, an ooze
to be sucked into any fissure
provided under the darkness in the sea
known as silence. Each helix of goo

was spat out again as a thing,
an artifact, a gadget, a gathering.

When the matter of lightness
and the matter of darkness coagulated
into genes. When the genes curlicued
into the spiraling chromosomes. When the atoms
of this and aspects of that drifted together.
Whenever they stuck,
and could not pull away,
whenever the putty of life
turned traitor and added
decomposition to the process.
Whenever the egg happened,
and after. When the chromosome.
When the gene. When the atom.
When the helix.
And when the idleness and the play.
And the anger and passion.
The inspiration. When the time
came to let loose the wild orca
into the sea. That was the moment
the darkness and the light ruptured,
like a prism.

The sky lit up. The earth crusted over.
The earth was divided into half dark,
half light. Into sky and earth. Land
and sea. And the body of the orca
black and white breached and splashed.
She opened her mouth, since
she had one, and shook her
four-inch teeth. And when she calmed,
the waters around her stilled,
and she breathed in two lungs full of air.
And then she began to sing. Everywhere

the song of the orca began to be heard.
The first noise of the earth an aria now.
Unboxed. At liberty. Abundant.

An ineffable tune,
lovely enough to be unending,
and final. The song of the orcas.
The light and the dark together.

This is the song
that has begun to disappear,
hushed, has moved toward silence
again. The song that might be saved.

## About Gratitude

Here I am away from home
in the company of women.
The ocean is at a loss for horizon,
but always comes forward
at the shoreline. And we

are in the company of women.
The assertion of waves washes the sand,
then relaxes, laying it down,
and taking it back to the heart.

In the company of women
glass floats and sand dollars, wet
with wave and rain, remain together
after the tide moves off. White froth
turns amber and thick,
like the language of gratitude.

And we are here,
just a small gathering of women,
writing under the gray clouds.
Tiny birds sing in the distance.

## Neap Tide Rising

The generosity of ocean waves delivers
tidal gifts to world travelers. Little white hats
on the horizon draw nearer and nearer.

Shorebirds gather together in the darkening dusk,
then disperse in the morning's weather. Seagulls
sail the drafts, and dip into the tips of waves.

Large logs prefer to travel alone in the storm,
unless they hang together as a solid
and dubious mass, a danger to dodge.

The cormorant, goldeneye and merganser
work the winter waves, a duty involving
the cold dimness of the depths, and also joy.

A seal's head rides the surface, blinks
at the wind, and thirsts for evergreen dew.
When it dives under, it never returns.

Otter tails rise up, too, and
then plunder under the crest
of the sea-gray table.

The wistful voices of the dead wash
ashore in the storms, an eternal chorale
singing the holy tones of stones.

The eagle sings with the awe of little girls,
that high and gleeful pitch. While the sea watches her
children, she dreams of her own lost mother.

## Arguing with Rumi

> *When you do things from your soul,*
> *you feel a river moving in you. A joy.*
> —Rumi

The soul is a heavy river,
a wide and muddy river,
a thick river
filled by the mountains,
and the drainage
of cities, and
the little drizzles.
Not joy. Not happiness.
But the soul working,
and working,
with elation and deep sorrow,
becoming its own truth.

## The New Poem

Whiteness everywhere, and more
snow on the way. The ice underfoot recalls
a line of letters, a syntactical arabesque.

*C'est la vie.* The pen
is the almighty; the paper
the flaccid supplicant.

It is already written and agreed.
The ice-clad muse has thawed.
She is dancing with the snowman.

A stack of words is afire.
The flurries are sizzling. She's
the expired skater of rhyme.

She holds the square peg like
a dowsing rod. Italics form a verbose river
of madness—the silt of sanity awash.

*Toodle pip, and I'm off.*
Darkness is overcome by dawn. The lord
and thy lady of London have already fallen

into the rot of the scribbling river—
musty, stark and acrid, the simmering gist.
Let us lie down. Let us imagine.

## Bearing Notes

> *People seem not to see*
> *that their opinion of the world*
> *is also a confession of character.*
> —Ralph Waldo Emerson
> *The Conduct of Life (1860)*

Here are the directions.
Be sure to have your pen
and journal ready at all times.
Follow your route thoughtfully.
Be precise.

Upon starting out, know enough
to follow a simple path. Look for one
that promises to reach a small wood
where cedars and wild rose might grow.

Your first attempt should be
in mid-afternoon when the sun
is particularly cruel. If you must,
squint until your eyes close.
Start walking your chosen trail.
Always step toward the most welcoming
route until it breaks into patterns—
of color or stripe, scent or texture.
Take notes. Record everything.

When you reach the woods, leave
the path. Find your own way.
Mosses and brambles will become
your Braille. Don't trip in this place—
you'd think someone dear will catch you.
Instead, you'll fall onto the scab of the earth
whose breath is scented with
blackberry and nettle. Be still.

Most likely you will not be harmed.
When you wish, move on.

In some hidden place will be
a grove dark with cedars and sword fern.
The scent of mildew and decay melt
into dirt like butter. Sticks, draped
with moss, scratch at the brown sky.
Be sure to make a journal entry here.
Take your time. Be thorough.
Then move on.

Further, will be a saggy barbed-wire fence.
Slip between its rusted points. The going
will be easier after. Listen for the sounds
of the animals, the birds, and insects,
and the brushing together of the plants.
There are languages being used. Some
nearly impossible to hear. Try
to understand and document
your impressions. When you
find a dry spot, stop and sit.

It is difficult to speak now. The voice
becomes a silent thrumming.
Rest and breathe until night falls.
Under the stars every strand of grass
carries a shard of moon. The grating
of branch on branch is a lullaby
you may sleep to. If you choose this time
to go, listen for the whistle of wings overhead.
They will not belong to angels.

Breathe deeply—even the scent of pain
is harmless. Somewhere, you'll hear
water carrying away the grit
and debris of your thoughts.

## Homage to Josef Albers

There, there is a square
in a square
in a square.
All in another.

One small yellow square calmly
resides inside a yellow square
inside an orange square
inside an orange square—

like a cubist fruit basket,
a square meal, or
even a square mile
of Saturday's market.

But I prefer the yellow square,
with an orange square within
an orange square, all
holding solidly to the red.

The red means a lot
to me. The warmth
of it floating beyond
the brightest yellows.

The yellow and the oranges
together, supporting the red.
This is something important.
No blues. No greens. Nor purples.

When the yellow dandelion
and the honeyed bee
pass between them
an orange hue—that is

an ardent support of red.
If this were another state,
red would be exactly
the same as green.

But we are talking
about the square root
of yellow here. The answer
is simple once you pass

the orange and get
to the heart of being.
The gray horse in the pasture
ignores the browsing deer

while the sun sets beyond
the blackened evergreens.
And then suddenly a sky
of yellow and orange cradles red.

The square of red, so small,
and brilliant as a hummingbird's
chin, creates enough space
a simple color may express love.

## Mona's Boredom

When Mona Lisa
came into this life,
she yawned. For weeks
and months, she yawned.
Because she was bored.
Because this life disappoints.
Because books were just catching on.
Because of the multiple and
monotonous masquerade parties.
Because there was no such thing as ice cream.
Because of the relentless cutenesses
of kittens, puppies and rabbits.
Because of the long lines at the market,
at the pastry shop, and even the ducklings
who waddle behind the duck.
She yawned as she grew.
She yawned widely for years.
She yawned because the future was already foretold.
Because water always falls from the pump.
Because there is always someone fighting
in the streets, in the dark, under the moonlight.
Because her boyfriend kissed too hard.
Because flowers are not forever.

But one day,
when she sat thoughtfully
in front of a painter
who painted her big hands,
and her parted hair,
and the folds of her dress,
and the long journey behind her,
she happened to smile a little
because of the light above the clouds,
because of the sound of brush on canvas,

because of the painter's humming,
and the empty frame waiting,
and the sudden gasp,
and the permanence
of that moment.

## The Metaphysics of Figure & Ground

First there is the wine glass.
Empty. Of course it is.
There are two people
who are looking at each other,
noses almost touching.
The glasses between them
still empty. Or are they now
completely full, a spicy
white wine filling it
to the brim? The people
are arguing. A prism
of pessimism shines
like crystal between them.
Things are looking up.

Then there is the chicken.
It came second. Definitely
not first. The egg has been around
long before the bird first
imagined itself. Even the frogs
sing about the long strings
of pearls, the clear globes
of other worlds lost across
the universe of their pond.
How did the egg become
the standard-bearer of life?
And the insects? We know
they are attracted to the flora
because they are jealous
of the seed. This eats them up.
They sow their eggs
in the ground like gardeners.

Near the end, we always wonder
*what is life anyway? Who are we?*
*Is this some kind of joke?*
We covet our lives, this split second
of eternity, more than anyone
else's spouse or house or horse.
The past hangs from the left hand,
future on the right, no end in sight
on either side. If life is the figure,
eternity is the ground. Look
a little too close, and we see
what we want to see, don't we?
Tip your head a little
and it's gone. We'll never know
for sure. But let us guess
for a moment
and another.

## Janitor of the Labyrinth

My quarters are centered in the middle
of the maze. Each evening, an hour
past dusk, my broom-cart echoes
into the corridor. If I keep one eye
on the right wall, the labyrinth
becomes a kind of sphere, always
turning in on itself, so
I can return to where I began.

My broom sweeps every corner
throughout the long nights. Often,
the kindly stars light my way.
But even during the blindness
of moonless, cloud-filled nights,
experience shows the way.

A lost soul or two will
wander up in the darkness.
They are always a bit terrified,
confused, often weeping. I give them
silent signals to follow.
If they complain that the sweeping
and picking-up of refuse
dropped along the aisles
is too slow, I am tempted
to lose them. But if I do,
I generally have to scour
up their fusty parts
the next evening. Sometimes,

I run into them again. They
may be angry and shout hysterically,
fingers pointing. My response
is simple—wordless, I sweep

them to the side until they
are scrabbling along the walls
behind me, the dust causing them
to cough and sneeze. They are quieter
that way, and more complacent.

Near morning, I push the broom-cart
up a high ramp, and dump it
over the side. This is a job I love.
From the rim of the labyrinth,
the landscape is endless,
like an ocean.

If stragglers trail behind me until
morning, they will see the beauty
of the sun streaming over
the tall walls—mists and rainbows
refracting, dancing. This
makes them exceedingly happy,
though the Minotaur
will be lurking nearby.

By morning, the labyrinth clean,
I always arrive safely to my door.
I go inside, eat, then sleep,
and dream of the horizon line
visible after I've dropped my holy
collection of filth and ugliness.
I waken to the sound
of cloven hooves on cobbles.

## The Door

When a door closes, a window opens in a house that is falling apart. Sorry, but that's the truth. Take a look at the door, but not too long. The window has already let in a chickadee, which is now in the kitchen eating crumbs off the birthday cake. The window, still open, and the cat is out looking for mice. What a day! All winter, the crack down the middle of the door lets the sun shine through from noon until one. Looks like lightning. Too bad the sun doesn't spread its warmth in here. Not with the window open and the long crack in the door. The drafts require a sweater every day except in July and August. Sometimes two, especially if that Nor'eastern is blowing down from Canada. When the window gets shut, the door creaks open again. This blasted drafty house. This time of year, hot tea near the window gets a scrim of ice when left on the sill too long. Look, a stray dog has come in the door, and peed on the leg of the coffee table. The chickadee has roosted on the couch. It likes the floral pattern, as it is pulling up threads to make a little nest. The dog joined the bird on the couch, but it now smells the birthday cake and runs to the kitchen, nose in the air. By mid-morning, I've chased the dog out the front door, covered the cake with a pot, shooed the chickadee out the window, and slowly lowered the window so as not to upset the balance between draft and stagnant air, and now I'm looking for the cat. So, yeah, I've been busier than heck, and haven't gotten a thing done today. Would ya please shut the door?

## A Comparison With or Without an Eagle
*after a poem by Brigit Pegeen Kelly*

Wind. Wind from the north. Canada. The grasses
green in their fields. Isn't the luster of gold inlaid
on their blades burden enough? Isn't the stiff resistance
of stalks the fix? Robins and waxwings revere the red berries
of mountain ash. Revere the practice of flight.

*Fly across the hemisphere. Fly above the hours. Fly,
fly through gray skies full of storm and the instinct of blue.*

This is how the mind
learns home, and home—tethered to the wing—
will sometimes burst into flame, as happened just yesterday,
breaking the untempered glass of fate. Fate
is not unjust. It is a routine custom among the living.
Fate knows the dance steps, and how to fit the shoes,
whether stilettos or sneakers, go-go boots or bare feet.
Go ahead, don the shoes. Test the walk like
a great blue heron, a cheetah. Don't forget—your conscience
doesn't count anymore. The second guess
is where the dancer trips.

*Wait. Walk. No Shoes, No Shirt, No Service.
Please Do Not Feed The Birds* and *Floss Every Day.*

But the rabbit dashes up the path.
Runs flat out on the path across the open field. Disappears
without paying the tab, without kissing the dog,
or cleaning up after the wag, leaves it for the torrents
to untangle. Jumped its puny scruff down the non-
returnable hole. Even today, bits of fur float on the breeze.
They are souvenirs. And they are stars.
The glittering eternity above us and below.

## Will of the Children

We were alive and rising skyward,
our childhoods the helium of life.

When oxygen thinned to nothing,
we learned to fly. Our feathers were iron

and held us miraculously aloft.
Then came the bullets

whizzing past. And the notification
from gravity that we must sink

or fail. Each breath became
a prize. Each drop of blood

a claim to our pasts. Our ancient
thoughts moldering in public.

An embarrassment. A shame.
We took it as our duty to heal,

to believe each injury
would be remembered,

would be an education
for our subsequent future.

Time will tell, perhaps,
if the heavens will

ever embrace us again.
We've sewn hope tight

to our jackets, next
to the golden buttons.

## This is the Way It Doesn't Work

I have just gotten off the phone.
The light around me is peaceful,
medicinal, which tends to help.
The phone, set in its cradle,
is like a baby, and I
its negligent mother. I'm still
giving the phone the evil eye.

Days like this force us
to understand *irrational*
is the new *rational*—
like being refused a bank refi—
one that would save us
a couple hundred a month.
But, we're told, we don't quite
make enough money for such
a request. Assets don't count these days.
That makes sense to someone.

Not me though.
There are times when a slug
is a sock. Pow!
I found two left
in the dryer this morning.
Slugs,
not socks. They must have crawled
in through the window.
This somehow makes sense.

I stare out an upstairs window
as breezes blade through the sunlit
grass, and all that is bright out there
in the pasture's stark sanity. A bird

smacks into the window. Bam!
Startled. It and I. A robin
and the robbed.

The window is narrow and tall,
like a supervisor. I turn around,
because I can't face it anymore.
This is rational.
But so is that bird on the ground.
Thousands of robins throw themselves
at windows every year, until
muddy streaks are spattered with blood.
Is it lust, or territory they're after?
Unwavering—they go on
till the end. They thrive on this
routine. How staunch of them.
Even drunken birds, filled to the beak
with a greed for post-ripe berries, perform
a constant defenestration of themselves.
They are one with the wall,
a transitory arrangement
among the windows. Even those
generally stable cedar
waxwings fail and fall.
This can be good
only for illustrators, biologists,
and feral cats.

This is not the way we see it:
We turn, and walk in another
direction whenever we can.
We are brilliant as those little
robot vacuum cleaners, who suck
everything in their paths until
they bounce into an obstacle.

Like them, we turn our backs
on all we've done,
and run off to someplace else.

But, I've turned back toward the window
now, and I see that the robin
is standing up, has gotten his wind,
shaken his head, and is off, flying—
has survived.

The phone rings, and I reach for it.
I pick it up, and ask, *Hello?*
This is not the way things work.
This is just the way they happen.

## Lines

It's mid-September.
Already the grasses have dried,
and broken in the wind. Here,
in the salt marshes of the Salish Sea,
shallow lines, harrowed for decades,
delineate saltwater blue
from yellow blades, a complement
of wet to dry. Clouds reflect
between the rows of harvested corn,
and I can't remember
ever seeing anything so calm.

Then, in the distance,
a young hunter's shotgun.

## Ode to the Beer-Colored Moon

*The Eclipsed Red*
Our moon is a hermit crab,
ruthless and bitter.
He is in pursuit of a lavish vessel,
which he will pirate
as his new hidey-hole.

At last, this florid moon backs
into a plain brown bottle—
a burbling lunatic who looks
to protect his underbelly,
while his burgundy glove
grasps at anything dark.

*Imperial Moon*
This windy evening our moon
becomes a torpedo that soars
through black sticks for hour
after bellowing hour. Just
before dawn, she cozies up
to the sun, filthy
and bitter still.

*Waning Crescent*
Yellow, the moon
is the flavor of dandelion,
biting the throat,
bruising both tongue
and tonsils, a breath
not quite good enough.

*Sunday's Summer Ale*
The golden halo
of a honey-colored moon,

smells holier-than-thou, which
isn't so great. A few shabby holes
in the clothes tell the tale.
Plus, the leavings of mice.

### The Bees Wax Gibbous
The new and ready-to-use
moon has training wheels
that buzz like bees. Flashy,
plastic strips trail behind
blowing in the breeze.

### Last Quarter
Blind, yet quick as a kick,
a foul round shadow
moves across the yard,
and there is a sound—
a back-of-the-mouth
giggle—a cousin lost in the dark.

### Hefty Moon
We quench our thirst with
the acrid moon. Savor
the strong, rosy floral,
its hint of honey. How about that
scotchless peat, with its finished
silken texture, the congruence
of burnt sugar? We write poems
about the moon because of all that.

### Full Moon
"Love the glow, old boy,"
you shout to the sky. Golden,
the lucky moon burns
behind a thin curtain of clouds.
You praise its sheen, so startling,

like the scent of grapefruit
hanging tight to the charcoal trees
in the night. Surprisingly tart!

### The Waning Porter
A darkling moon
sips ivory foam slowly all night,
bark-sweet and creosote-warm,
a dull glow fades away
like a wounded hound.

The last sliver of moon
in the morning
tastes of molasses
and blueberries.
Hunger follows,
voracious and fierce.

## Can You Hear Me?

The red moon, the cold stars,
and the uncertain planets.

I began asking quietly,
"Is anybody out there?" but

the sun vaporized the words
inches from my mouth. I asked again,

louder this time. But it wasn't enough.
I spoke into a microphone,

and the stars seemed further than ever.
Some disappeared from view.

"Can you hear me out there?"
I said into the radio waves.

Static crackled into each letter,
disintegrated entire words.

The distance from here to another life
seemed out of reach. Am I alone?

Next, I tapped out a coded message
on a sending unit, and I believe

my words are finally on their way: white
noise vanishing into a grim, distorted hole.

It's been days, maybe weeks. So far,
no response. Meanwhile, I continue

my search for other means of understanding
the strange landscape of language—

the oceanic pitch and swell,
the mountainous amplitude,

and especially the quakes
and eddies of silence.

If you can hear me, what
will you say?

## Ode to the River Willow

You sit beside the pond near me,
and you're reaching across
to the other shore, too. I've watched
your thicket of arms tangle closer
together for decades as though
constructing a better home,
a beefy defense, a shield. Each spring,
thin shoots erupt from your wild-eyed limbs.
They are thin, pliable, and strong.

You've sat beside this pond
for decades while wood ducks nested
in the cave of your shoreline root-ball.
In your wooden womb, moist secrets grew,
one ovoid casing at a time.

When I put my cheek against a branch,
there's a calm gesture from within,
like the movement of breathing. But
I know it's the caress of the wind.

During recent winters, your impenetrable
duck-nest cave ruptured, spread apart,
like legs opening to the sky, like you
were giving birth, but to what? The time
for birth is also the time for death:
of the wide sanctuary you became,
of your torso brandishing arms
that hold the skies at bay,
of the bared roots whose teeth
still grip the earth.

This spring, my chain saw
took the dead branches
from your hollowed trunk,
while green life sprung from you.
Each new leaf the frog's song. Each twig,
the song bird's perch. You roll over.
Shrug off the old. Create a new stronghold.
I can hear the wood ducks
flying this way. The mallards.

## Abandoning Spring

Just because the ditches overflow
and the nor'easter winds along the shallows,
and twigs of cedar and alder skirt the moody path
along the road, and memory is a wonky dialect,
the division between this year and last is minor.

No need for an explanation. Idling daffodils
shout obscenities from underground, impatient
as they are to hear the glow of their name
in the misty air. They are the small haunters
of large dreams that are only experienced once.

## In the Beginning

Darkness—fleeting streaks
of white on black.
The small seeds of light
stretch as dancers do—
outward, then in and up.

I've seen tulips dance like this
in the rain, their shadows muddy
and tangling in the light.

If a drenched white tulip
could sing, her voice might sound
like the squeak of rubber soles
echoing across a dance floor.

### I Thought I Saw Your Underwear
*with a few lyrics from "This Little Light of Mine"*
*by Harry Dixon Loes*

You were curled in the shadows
under a row of bush beans.

You had a candle. Don't
worry. What you were doing

will never see the light.
Not by these lips anyway.

The bag. The stolen beans. The startled
moment when you noticed someone saw you

sprawled there in the garden, singing:
*This little light of mine, I'm going to let it shine.*

Higher! *This little light of mine.* "It's all mine," you said,
between verses. "It's *all* mine." *Hide it under a bushel?*

*No!* Though a candle on a stick is out
of fashion, it liberates the most

romantic light, but that is all.
Let your light shine like fire,

like the sun when the rain has quit,
like the women who dance beneath a deluge

of moonlight. Even you can become
that beautiful. A simple candle

can make that happen. Light it
and pray. But here you are, lying

in the dirt amongst the bush beans.
Tell us the truth, dearest one.

Be honest, and I won't let slip
that I saw you in the beans today.

Your underwear showing like fire.
*Don't let Satan [blow] it out!*

You're going to *let it shine,*
*all the time, let it shine.*

## The Lawn Mower

The guy with the mower starts
and stops the thing all morning and
into the afternoon. It drives me crazy.
Blue smoke puffs from the machine
while he whistles for his dog.

He shoves that mower
in long, dusty rows. He makes love
with the sunlight, with the blunt edging
around the shrubs, with all the falling
leaves, each in their turn,
then gabs with the man next door
until I can stand no more.

He turns the picnic table
upside down, and sits on the ground,
eats a lunch of leftover walnuts and sage.
He grins widely, then wanders the bushes
searching for his custom-sized gloves.

Look. The grass glistens green
and grows some more.

His dog has disappeared
down the road days ago,
and won't be coming back.
I know this in my secretive way.
The mower makes another round,
growling and cursing.
He'll never find his gloves.
I ask no forgiveness.

**Freeze Frame**

In warm weather, stunted black ants
march briskly across the slab table
under the cottonwoods.

If I set my journal down, or
even a pen, anywhere near one,
it will halt, become immobile:

a minuscule pismire who freezes
in place—sometimes for over
a minute it will stand stock-still

like the tiniest statue in the world.
I thought it dead, and prepared
to flick it off when, abruptly, the thing

starts up again as if it had just
come to, suddenly remembered
the kettle left on the burner, or

heard someone yell "Green light!"
And off it goes again, the mechanical ant,
as though nothing had ever happened.

## Ode to the Cherry Tomato

Little fruit, tiny vegetable
pulled from a tangled, sticky branch—

picked ripe—a surprise here,
even in September—the tomato
is the flesh of physical faith.

We believe each spring
that this will be the year
of the Early Girl and the Beefsteak
ripening on the vine.

To pluck the ripened one
shall be followed with
a ritual in honor of the red
and the smooth, the juicy.

Let the tough skin
entertain the teeth
and tongue. Let go
the wonder of spring
to the quench of autumn.
Bite down slow,
receive the tang
and squirt.
The rapture.

## Exactly Verbatim, an Unsung Opera: The Summary

### Act I

All wounds have a stake. The bet
is waged by a fidgety fingered nurse.
The good dog of passion is spurned
by the lover who whispers commands.
There is a tussle toward the end
of this first act. It doesn't go well.

### Act II, Scene I

A torch carried into battle as a bayonet
leaves one weaponless and spotlit.
The messenger shoots twice,
and misses. Lucky dog. A brilliant red
is smudged across a gray panorama—
nobody can take their eyes off it—
a monochromatic photograph stolen
from living pigment. WWII planes
go down with honor and smoke.
Dancers surround a fire.
Someone is singing. [fades out]
The sound of dancing
continues on the darkened stage.

### Act II, Scene II

The entire body of people
tug on an apron string,
each part desperate for the others.
The cry for help is in a baritone voice:
Oh, mother, sing the aria again
in the tongue of angels. Sing
through the hole in my heart.
The mouser is then freed from the pouch.

He injests the stone and the fluff,
swallows the tripe whole—ah,
but he lets the wren take wing.

### Act III, Scene I
Scene begins with a hacking cough,
the sound of a bottleneck sliding along guitar
strings, and a magazine of bullet casings
dropped on the desk. The cockeyed
sea dog is sitting up, begging.
He is swamped, and at the mercy
of a three-legged table.

### Act III, Scene II
A sailing ship heaves in the storm.
The captain is shouting:
Lash down the chicklings.
Let the molting fowl swarm as one
across the quilted bulk of the sky.
The life of the hero is a reflection,
a lonely passenger on the eye
of the hen. There is a large mirror
behind hero and hen.

### Act III, Denouement
The stage is empty, except
for the sound of thunder
and the presence of a cannon
on the loose. Watch out.
It's curtains.

## Cascadia: a Love Song in Seven Parts

*From a Distance*
Dusk, and the tide is out.
Dark island bluffs stand stark
against the citrus sky.
A luminous echo has fallen
across the flattened bay.

The eagle and the moon
ignore each other, resting
in the trees above
a complicated conduit of kelp.
Communication between the Salish Sea
and the Cascade forest is happening.
Let's study this

for a moment. The mountain trees
wave their cones and needles, scraping
the skin of the sky. Low tide, and long fronds
sprawl across the beach to telegraph
a message in the sand. You can see it.
If you're careful, and take your time,
you might even begin to hear
the scratching of light static
in the distance.

*The Red Star*
It's noon, and
a starfish is dancing
in the shadows.
The delicate legs
of the blood star elegantly poised
in the slowest ballet on earth.
Above this down-tempo

performance, even further
above the bluest sky, the hottest
stars in the universe echo
this indulgent radiation of arms.
Such a leap as this
has no equal.

### The Mountain Ash

Winter, and the Mountain Ash
is bare. Grey branches yearn
upward, sated with sap.

The orange fruit of August
turns crimson in September,
just as my heart darkens
when you leave. A sour berry.

When the Rowan thickens
with robins and waxwings,
the harvest is quick.
Your muddy footprints
will soon be filled
with red leaves and berries.

### A Report

Last night, between
the sporadic chaos of the coyotes,

and the drumming jazz
from the yellow-bellied bull frogs,

a great horned owl sat
quiet in a weathered pine,
blinking.

### The Updraft
Today, I am the color
of ash floating before
a weakened sun.
All day I turn over and over
in the air, changing direction
as though I were undecided,
and finally, here I am
settling down
into a smoky corner,
music burning
all around.

### Coronis Fritillary
The yellow butterfly takes
a dubious route to get
no place in particular.
Her wings carry the spots
of a gambler. A little hesitation,
a bright breeze, and
there goes this restive creature
embarking on a wavering flight
which will take her farther
than possible to get
exactly where she meant to go.

### As the Full Moon Rises
Slow and heavy,
she comes,
breaking the black
line of the mountains.

Pale yellow
and colossal,

she struggles through
a snarl of jagged branches,
only to transform above the horizon
into a diminutive white dot.
She radiates flawlessly
with the exhaustion of perfection
and the labor of letting go.

## Unraveling the Gossamer Silk of Thought

The hand-sewn butterfly net flaps
at half-mast again today.
The monarch has taken leave.

Frilly ruffles on the wings of angels
are gathered together—applied
by a desperation of long basting stitches.

The languorous sloth is the animal version
of a hammock. His only vice is that
he embroiders lies within his lining.

Fragments of the mind, those brooding rags,
routinely snarl and fray like well-worn flags,
like teeth that snap and unsnap in the dark.

The hat I wear is of a fabric dusty with barn webs,
and has a shiny bobble. Its seams are filled
with the fabrications of dissent.

When the sewing machine backtracks the final seam,
I reach for the iron and steam the wrinkles flat,
scorch the linen. If the hem is uneven, let it be.

The strains of "Ava Maria Stella" help our untimely warp
and weft—give us shelter beneath tattered wings
as we weave toward our half-sewn unseemly end.

The silk worm binds itself with a fine filament
over four thousand feet long. The miracle
is not the thread, but the concentration.

*Letter for the
Day After Tomorrow*

## Letter for the Day After Tomorrow

Is this the life we dreamed of? Cold
cereal every morning. Coffee. A sandwich at noon.
Gray daylight pouring through every window.

Both of us reading different sections of the paper.
Afternoons, we spend pondering ourselves.
Wondering what hat to wear. Boots today?

We're poets acting like poets, so tragic
and obvious. Sparrows tap at our window, begging
for seed. Spindly maples wave behind them, frantic.

Everywhere we go, the motion makes us sick.
We stop for a beer in the evening, a ritual we enjoy,
tasting the bitter ales. Our life seems better for the moment.

As though things have gone as planned. And then an apparition
appears on the horizon, a ghostlike bird with raptor wings.
But it disappears quickly into the clouds, and at last

when a bit of sun streams through, things brighten to orange.
With the days so strangely normal, and the breezes
light, night begins quietly, a symphony, beautiful,

though slightly out of tune. That one violin. You turn out
the lights. Darkness pushes us into our bedroom.
The maples shake red sticks at us.

Another naked tragedy is happening.
And the poets look into the moonlit yard,
whispering sad lines to each other.

## Walk Away Wisely
*for Denise Snyder*

A slim path drizzles through
the evergreen forest. You're
on it. The greenest moss drips
slowly from cedars. Lichen
nurses quietly like a baby
from everything made of wood
you can see. Even the rocks
carry lichen on their backs. Ferns
cut their way through the tangled trees.
This is an environmental metaphor
you'd best decipher soon.
There are rules

to abide by here. Like never run
from a bear. Just walk away, as though
you're in grade school, trying
to avoid a bully. If you can
sneak away from that deep,
dark bear, all will be well. It's good
to resist the urge to run from a predator.

It is raining. "Dry" is a simile
for "never." It is a joke no one gets.
Insects are scarce for now,
having scurried into their dens—
fissures in the bark— or
they've burrowed under the dampening dirt.
They will rise again soon enough.
May it rain forever and ever.

Sometimes, danger is beautiful.
Stay away from the pretty deer.
And more-so, the moose. Don't forget

how to run like heck
if one chances upon you.
At the sight of a big bull moose,
you'll become that strong.
You'll learn to plant a large tree
between you and the horse-sized bovine.

Run in circles around that tree
until you've made the world's
most impenetrable moat.
Fortunately, it is still raining.
Love the rain.

## The Weather of Transition

This afternoon, ashen gray clouds
sulk into deep, charcoal skies.
Wind from the south
eddies with the north
like some sort of game.
But we know it isn't.

Except for the one chickadee
wiping its beak on the alder,
the birds are black today,
no matter the species.
They toss themselves
every which way
between the prickly trees.
They are wild,
and solicit abandon.

People all over the planet leave their homes
in terror, come back like sheep, bleating.
The lost losing the shepherd; the shepherd
following a trail to the other side of the mountain.
Also lost.

Like bullets, suddenly anger
births itself from lovely, copper shells.
People are foolish as can be today—
doing the addition of stupidity
through multiplication.

For some reason,
we can understand this.
We are so far gone
that we can only see

the violently beautiful sunset
turn dark as night.
As we close our eyes, we hope
this is a promising sign.

## First Darkness

A moonless winter night colors everything
a single shade of black. A barred owl
out back in the cedars fluffs itself
against the cold. The scent of wood smoke
and the probable snow drifts in my window
though winter's nearly done.

It's a little after five when
the owl hoots eight times. Then
her deep *hoo-waah*. Light begins
to open slow as lotus petals.
The waning of darkness
is like waking from the dead—
if you can imagine—
which takes time, as the trees
grow old while it happens.

When the cowardly glow
of morning arrives, not one frog
is bold enough to speak. Yet, there
goes the owl again, in the first dim
shot of dawn, hooting. Her streaked feathers
run down from the beak's sharp crescent
to the dark curve of her insightful talons.
The pussy willow's yellow-gray fuzz
adds ironic color to the landscape.

Because the grief of darkness is reluctant
to leave too soon, the mice and rabbits,
possums and raccoons, impatiently rustle
in the underbrush. The sparrows
and nuthatches cling like ice to their twigs.
The grit of the gravel under a lone car
growls up the road. Then more silence.

Why is it that, at a certain point
on the daily fulcrum,
the light opens so decidedly?

Once the day is broken open, the owl
of the woods disappears into
a pocket of tree. The others
begin to scurry and stop,
scurry and stop—they pick and eat,
gather and hide, threading themselves
around the lowest of branches,
large bursts of fern. A lousy seed
will catch their eye, like a spark.

The sun begins to change
to golden orange—a trace of warmth.
Spring is in the wings, though the days
turn still colder. Maybe soon, we'll grasp
the owl's wonderment as the new claw
of the moon begins to rise.

## Spotting an Owl in a New-Mown Field

It's midnight, mid-summer, with the small moon waning,
but we peer into the unknown distance anyway.

The thin curve of the moon delivers
a convenient spark that dimly lights the way.

The bright scent of hay
scatters across the muted pasture.

Broad wings, engineered for silence,
carry the dart of an owl, who drops and rises again.

Small squeak. Fringed wing and downy body
calm the turbulence in the crook

of talons. Discerning black
from gray, we organize

the jumble of newly cut rows—
a mouse from a hole, rabbit

from tuft, the silver glitter cast
across this chasm of night

and millions of tiny stars
sparkling across the dewy field.

## The Mole

Only the mole truly believes
he's made a mountain.
And when he struggles out from under,
he believes he sees God,
that blinding light,
that tender warmth.
He hath granted the lowly mole
the comfort of life underground,
tunneling always toward his dreams.

The mole welcomes all
with enormous hands extended wide.
*Praise God who made these mighty paws*
under the brightness of heaven's stars
*to do their work tilling the earth.* A mole
has toiled in the soil for an eternity,
each heap emerging as an early morning
surprise. Who can say for sure
if the scruffy foothills and
the high blue mountains
aren't the mounds birthed
wholly by the passionate labors
of the burrowing mole?

Teach yourself
the handshake of a mole—
an earthy, encompassing grasp,
poking pink and callused,
like a thumb from an elegant
black-velvet glove.

## Unless It Rains

We'll go outside on a sunny
afternoon to sit on a bench
to watch the birds, or the changes
in the color of the light. Very pleasant.
Happy to be there anytime at all,
unless of course it rains,
unless it begins to sprinkle
as we step outside,
unless there's the threat of a deluge,
with drops so close together
they could become a portable waterfall.

Or maybe we'll be caught out there
in a heavy spring shower because
rain is unpredictable and ornery.
With no hat or umbrella at the ready,
our hair becomes plastered to our heads.
Tendrils dripping like faucets.
Our coats soak through to our shirts,
and then to our skin. The bare earth
will grow sudden puddles. Under these
circumstances, we should run for cover
to avoid the embarrassment of this insult
from nature, of the excessive loads
of swampy laundry in our futures,
and of the possibility of melting
like a sugar cube or a wicked witch. That is

unless we happen to look up
and see the rain as it rushes toward us.
Unless we see how each drop plummets
to earth as though nothing can stop it,
and nothing really can until
it lands on your waiting face.

Besides re-quenching the thirst of the earth,
and bringing life into every single cell
on this planet, isn't this what the rain is for:
to elate the unsuspecting? The fact
of the standing puddles, and your
saturated leather shoes, should not stop you
from stepping onto the purest dance floor
nature can provide. *Go ahead! Try it.*
The splashes will be sensational and rapturous.
You may never have the opportunity
to succumb to such a joy like this again.

## Reckless Grace

Last night, as I knelt beside the bed,
I couldn't help but notice the ache
in my knees, and my wrists, fingers,
and heart. So I whipped through

my little prayer to ease my knees.
It's funny, isn't it, how when you pray,
you either close your eyes tight,
bow your head and put your palms
together at your chin, or you
open your eyes wide, hands
clenched into wrestling fists, and
you look up, pleading to the skies,
or the ceiling, as it turns out.
Still, don't you imagine
you're seeing heaven?

But there are times when,
though you close your eyes
and become quite thoughtful,
you sneak a peak to witness
the faithfulness of others—
those who close and bow,
and those who keep their eyes
open to the heavens. It is then
that you discover those who
also glance around the room.
Each of you committing
another tiny shame, a faithlessness.
But we pray, each of us,
in our own way. Don't we?

It's a wonder to rush headlong
into grace. To reach out

to each other in love. To ride
that fast horse to heaven.
To jump into the open sportster,
and race along the countryside,
pedal flat to the floorboard.
To jump from the airplane,
pull the cord, and dive, finally,
into the deep blue sea,
graceless as we are.

## The Green Pear

On the sunlit sill, a green pear
begins to blush. It's been ripening
for days. Forever. The pear
was picked too soon, for fear
it would turn to mush. But in fact,
the meat is hard as stone.

Wrapped in paper and tucked
into darkness, the cruelty
of a sour pear sweetens in time.
But this is a waste of beauty.

The pear tree grows in the foothills
where cool rains wash
the orchard clean. The grove
is like a close-knit family,
and follows the valley, as does a river.

There, the air opens to the sound of flickers
calling, a fitful knock on wood.
Sunlight sugars the pear, a ladle of luster.

## A Day of Thrush Songs

A light breeze, the cottonwood branches
bristle and groan. This is the first gesture
of the day. When I open a book,

a yellow leaf with seven points appears.
A vine maple, bright yellow, and it means nothing
deeper than that. It's May,

and everything joyous is bathed
in green or absolved with gray.
Dark clouds gather and deepen;

torrents every night.
By day, the aria of dandelion
and buttercup. There's a scraping

at the wall, like branch tips
or tiny claws. The sound is
out of sync with itself,

and, as it turns out,
is only a sparrow on the sill
scratching like a hen. For hours,

the gray Appaloosa
in the roadside paddock
has stood by the fence

and stared at the neighbor's house.
No one is home. The curtains drawn.
A chorus of thrushes whistles upward.

But there is no preparation
for the fallen one. No one will notice
the cold thrush beside the road. This is a deletion

of memory. On the hill,
still in sunlight, honeybees
hurry back to the hive.

## The Tardy Garden of Late June

Since early April, the rascally garden
has been stuffed with seeds, expecting.
Yet, only the peas and the weeds
have agreed to share. The rake

and the hoe have become true friends.
After weeks of heaping hills, laying rows,
poking holes, they are lying side
by side in the dirt, panting.

Lay your ear to the ground,
and you'll hear earthworms humming
through mud, laying out the lines
in hopes an anarchy of long hairy roots

will follow. Once the ladybugs
have landed on the underside
of every future leaf, the lettuces
will begin to pray for the kale

in their sad blue row. The carrots'
frilly tops will stake out the thin spindle
of orange beneath. They dig deep
as philosophers as they try

to make a point. The sudden hank
of potatoes will begin to write journals
full of notes underground
where the bok choy can't see.

But the rabbits can.
When they come up for air,
they put their wiggly noses
to the fence, biding time,

as they watch the rhythm of the sprinklers
embossing tear-like divots in the ground.
The riotous cotyledons will soon
be released, those two little leaves

opening in praise of the blue, blue sky.
This will finally give us the glimmer of faith
we were searching for. At dusk,
silence. The stage, set.

A rustle near the startled artichokes,
shimmers like light over the purple earth.
The tragic story of life begins.
The Green Chorus shuffles across the loam

and begins to sing. Woe to the aphids.
Rue the slugs. One can hear the eager
groan from the beets, the joyous earth parting,
the rumors spreading from seed to seed.

## What the Buzz is All About

A bumble bee flies low across the duff
like a harrier, the hawk who looks
for dinner in the mulch.

Low and lower she goes.
This is not about sweetness,
not about the waxen, nor
the repetition of hexagonal perfection.

The blundering bee is an aircraft
aiming for a flower, making a flyover
too risky to compensate for error,
her landing gear always down
and at the ready.

There are laws out there
to follow if one wishes to fly—
how many wing beats per second,
how wide the wing, how round
and fluffy must be the body
to achieve the ultimate flight.
Do not forget the weight capacity
of wing load. Remember
the precise amplitude of buzz
to waver over the laden blossoms.

This fuzzy bee's motto
has always been, "The humbler
the bumble, the bumbler
the bungle." She knows you know
exactly what she means.

## The Ant Hill Beside the Sweet Peas

*Spring*
A thatcher hill, busy
beside a barbed-wire fence,
rises from the ground,
rippling like wind on water.

Tall grass surrounds the mound,
blunt-tipped and brown. A patch
of sweet peas tangles alongside;
its tendrils winding and
unwinding, tighten further.

Red-headed ants with large bustles
mosey—they do not hustle—
across, and then down into
sporadic half-inch holes, which
are camouflaged and pocked randomly
over the dome. So many ants
teeming there, they become a crust,
the roofing tiles.

*Late Fall*
The wild sweet peas
have gone to seed. The pods,
once black and full, are twisted
spirals, emptied of fruit. The sun
moves behind a cloud.

The activity of the hill
is urban, a traffic jam. One ant
carries a piece of dry grass,
the end bent at an angle.
He pushes every ant he meets
out of his way. Another holds

a pine needle like a lance. The others
stay out of his way. There's one who
moves backward, struggling
with a large twig. Each ant ignores
this difficult task, and walks over
and along his burden with impunity.

Two get into a tug-of-war with
a tiny piece of brown grass.
When one finally lets go, the other
changes direction, marches past his adversary,
and dives down the nearest hole,
grass blade and all.

### The Seeds
The ants continue their struggles
farther from the hill. On the other side
of the nearest building, one thatcher
is carrying a white seed, while
another bears a particle of bark. They
are trying to find a pass over a long
green garden hose. They run quickly
with their loads, then retrace their steps,
and repeat the process. One finds space
enough beneath the hose, runs through
backward, turns and hurries off.

Three sweet pea seeds lying in a row
look like the body of an ant.

The other shinnies up a grass stem,
drops from the tip, and finds
himself atop the hose. He falls
to the other side. Both ants
hurry, paranoid and skittish,
toward the colony.

Over the middle of the mound,
a grass stalk leans in a graceful curve.
One ant, empty-handed, climbs
the stalk to its seedy end,
and jumps into a hole. The sweet
pea seeds, long past flowering,
are covered with damp
and desiccating leaves.

## The Pond Takes an Afternoon Nap

Hot sun is discouraged
from entering the pond
by a stand of cottonwood,
alder, the snarling wild rose
and blackberry. This barrier
is intent on success.

Shiny black water becomes a trance,
dreams of an upside-down world,
suspends leeches and dragonflies,
polliwogs, and tiny brown worms
who flex through the murk.
Everything dawdles here.

This pool breathes slowly:
a meditative inhale of shadow;
an exhale of mist. Effervescence
caresses the underside of each lily pad,
bubbles up to the gilt overlay of the pond.
Stability at the surface is acceptable.

The job of a water ouzel is to follow
a ripple to its end. When the tiny bird
slips into the water over its head, then
out, there is no note of embarrassment.

Finally, the late afternoon sun begins
to fade, leaving golden streaks of light
across the surface and the blades of cattail.

## The River Decides to Flood

The Nooksack decides to flood
this year in early November.
Why not, it thinks, being overdue
for a vacation—a quick visit
to the deeper areas past the brink
of the thin forests and decrepit barns.
Might be nice to get into town
once in a while. The fine silt-brown
water rises quiet during the night.
Lawns become faux lakes. Migrating
ducks and geese rest on the easy,
flat water, and dip for worms
and slugs to tide them over.

The river runs faster some
places than others. Flower beds
disappear. Gravel moves from one
driveway to the next. An elderly
mother slips into a current. The river,
enjoying its holiday, begs her
to come along. But her daughter
grabs the mother's coat, and
yanks her back safe to the bank.
Yes, this really happened!

The Nooksack doesn't even care,
and begins to waltz, happy with the flow
choreographed by the shore's weedy edge.
A child skips a rock halfway across
the river. When no one is looking,
the ripples disappear. This is the best joke
the river knows. When the Nooksack retreats

to its muddy banks, the year's soggy wilting
begins. The river gestures with rapid excess,
covets surplus eddies, and celebrates with
ribbons and streamers along its entire length.

## Bezoar of Spring

It's mid-spring. The winter winds
still blow, and the brink of rain
is ever-present. The ferns
are almost through
with the act of unfurling,
and the bleeding hearts
have suggestive green pods
hanging from wilted pink petals.
It's almost funny. The fruit trees
drop confetti across the lawn,
and the cottonwood coughs up
something resembling tiny fairies
who drown themselves
quick in the murky pond. This

is the time of year that smells
delicious. Everything is opening
or poking through, cracking.
Think of the dragonfly who
wriggles its head, legs, wings
out of a cramped carapace.
A miracle I'm glad
not to be part of.

The sun makes a few attempts
each week to elbow through
the shiny rain. Gives up.
Water everywhere. Puddles
empty and refill as though they
were lungs. But they aren't,
you know. This is just how
it happens around here

before the wart hog of summer
crawls out of the muck
in the ditch,
blinking.

## As Spring Marches Louder

Hold still, little sister.
Watch the sun
dial its way around the earth.
Keep your feet planted
in the grass.

With the wind blowing
like it is today, somehow
a large cardboard "L"
flew overhead like a kite
and landed in the pond.
It is red, and now flapping
in the breeze. There's nothing
for the geese to do but
quiver near the opposite bank.

Rains race and dawdle
like commuters. Daily,
they wash the trunks
of pines and maples, rattle
the gravel, doing the chores
to make way for the songbirds:
the tweedle of blackbird,
the golly-gee of chickadee.

As the early morning gasps,
trust me,
you'll see fog rolling in slow
over the unkempt pastures,
and notice slug breath
glistening like dew.

It'll be then you can't keep
from waltzing to the lofty green
melody of the frogs.

## Hummingbird Renditions

1.
My fork hovers above
the plate this evening
like an obsessed bird waiting
for nectar. I'm hungry
and impatient. I've never before
craved an aphid.

2.
Mountain meadows of early fall
brim with young hummingbirds.
They dive-bomb flowers
like potential peace activists.
Flower children.

3.
Hummingbirds are unmistakable.
However, discerning nuance
is necessary for female identification.
The young are simply
indistinguishable from each other.
Don't even bother.

4.
Hummingbirds are noted
as an aggressive species.
I wonder what happens
to the old ones?

5.
Yesterday, in the downpour, I saw
a mother hummer. She stood on tiptoe
beside her nest, and stretched
over the rim to poke

her darning beak into
the open mouth of a fat hatchling.
Rain poured around her.
The nest was protected
from rain by being positioned
precisely under a thin limb.

6.
Once, while
still in the crib, I was
a bird. Hovering.
I had a needle beak.

7.
True hummingbirdness is defined
by the ability to sit so still
that a nest made of spider silk,
decorated with lichen, and set
precariously
on the horizon of a branch,
will remain intact.

## Early One Morning

It's not always easy getting up
to squint all day toward sunset's fireball.

This time of year, even the mossy footpaths
have dried to dirt, and blow harmless

tornado bouquets. The scent of alder
mixes with the sweat of the horse who

is running uphill toward the forest vistas.
She churns her hooves as if every step

might be her last. Not like you think.
But like every step is her first, too.

Like this is the day that will be
the most important of her life.

Like she's taking you along
just for the ride.

## Moody Interruptions on a Nurse Log

I.
Not a great day. Not a great time.
But I found a good place in the woods:
A frog croaks in the underbrush.
A robin mocks him from a tree.
And the rabbit who rustles nearby
turns out to be a couple birds
telling lies from the brambles.

>The twinned sounds of an autumn leaf
>falling and a chain saw in the distance
>have the same intensity,
>   if the leaf is near enough.

I'm sitting in the crook
of an old nurse log that's done it's job.
My back against a trunk, four more cedars
ahead in a line. Mounds of branches
are looped and tangled. And I think
of practicing good handwriting, and fail
because I can't stop rushing. Dead branches
twist through dead trunks. There is no eraser.

>In the wide spread of a maple
>are the remains of a tree house
>our kids once played in. It's been falling,
>bit by bit, for several winters.
>Most of it decays at the root.
>The rest hangs akimbo,
>mossy and indelicate.

A cedar branch holds a curled birch leaf,
tan with expectations of autumn's abuse.

>The robin quit, but the frog takes up
>where the bird left off,
>and then stops just the same.
>It's a fine thing to sit alone
>when you're angry for no reason.
>Old dirt smells good.

II.
There's that frog again. The chain
saw's still chewing and a tractor
rambles further out. The forest
begins to smell like petroleum products,
but I don't feel like getting up. The trees
are quiet now. Do they notice when the sun goes down?
The wind tries not to disturb them,
so they are left to their formal meditations.
I sit here stewing.

>I think I see a fungus
>growing underneath a downed cedar.
>Being near-sighted, I could be wrong,
>but if I'm not, it's one of the biggest fungi
>I ever thought I saw.

Sword ferns grow here.
Next to this nurse log is a pair of old birches.
One clings to what's left of another rotted birch:
the live one surrounding the other,
while ducks whistle overhead.
The other birch leans away from them.

>There go the ducks again,
>and robins resume talking in the treetops.
>The chain saw is gone, but a dog
>barks in its place. The sun has set.
>I've not improved my penmanship.

I've grown tired of interruptions,
so I came out here, where I have interrupted the robins,
  frogs, trees, nettles, the sun and myself.
  It doesn't even matter. I plan to stay here
  until the colors all turn gray.

III.
There's a crashing in the brush
near the pond, moving this way. Probably a deer,
maybe two. Already gray is the only color.
Minutes pass, and the deer haven't come by.

  Instead a raccoon peers at me
  from just the other side of the cedars.
  A big one. Then a smaller coon
  arrives, and stands up behind the first
  to get a better look. I decide to leave,
  but where they're standing
  is the only way out. This tree
  I'm sitting under might be their home.
  I have to go. As I stand up to leave,
  a third raccoon is startled
  from the other end of the log I'd sat on.
  Another big one.

Because I'm standing,
both large raccoons hustle up
the trunks of nearby trees.
The little one stays where he is, growling.
I walk toward him, slow,
and he growls louder,
but begins to walk away, grumbling.
The raccoon in the nearest tree
slides down to the base, shuffles around,
and gets a good look at me while he hides
on the other side. It's getting dark

in the trees. The raccoons
want privacy, will accept
no interruptions.

        I make a leisurely
        beeline out of the woods.
        Maybe this day isn't so bad after all.

## The Glow of Petals

Oh, Pruner
of roses,

Creator
of hybrids,

Organizer
of beauty,

be generous
today.

Graft us
a new start.

The roots
of peace

grow thick
and deep—

radiant with
fertile devotion.

# The Drenched: A Creation Myth for the Pacific Northwest

*A duck knows something
You and I don't.*
—Theodore Roethke

### *Genesis*
During the downpour this morning,
a percussion of thunder entered my dreams,
and played me awake. Lightning spat
yellow sky. Rain scrolled down the windows.
Bits of moss, insect parts, and pine needles
stuck to the glass. The trees wielded
their branches in alarm.

I've learned so little
in all this time.

The furious crash of wind climaxed
like a symphony practicing the same score
over and over—Rachmaninoff, distracted
and depressed.

### *Carpenter of Arks*
The flood deepens. But this rain
doesn't make sense to me. It's been talking
crazy since eight this morning, and I've followed
every word.

I am about to burst. Water is creeping
above my calves, seeping
into my clothes. I've prepared
for disaster, but forgot my pocketknife,
don't own a bailing bucket.

The weight of rain overwhelms:
a watery train that hurtles down upon us.
This should be no surprise, but it is. Things
can always get worse. It's a rule made up by God.

Rain pelts the house—
another stoning.

### Revelation
There are no birds when it rains
this hard. They blink
out. Then blink back before it dries.

There are times when I can't make
out the trees across the yard. Distance
turns into a myopic blur of green,
an orange blotch.
It brightens under a yellow sky.

I am a bird. It is raining.

### Miracles
I wonder how wild things stay
dry in a deluge. Do they curl and sleep
in hidden places, tail over nose, and wait
until the rain slows? Or are they little gods
who dodge the drops? I may be wet
as a dog, but I've never met a drenched coyote.

The Great Blue Heron flies low
over the bay, tilts her wings,
and sinks to the slough. She wades
high as her thighs, a hunting lunatic, moves
slow and serene as Nefertiti,

then stops, tilts her head to search
the water, as though she's found her prey.
She pauses there, neck akimbo, then moves on—
the queen who never eats.

   **Belief**
There are secrets out there I can't
begin to guess. Beneath every rock
resides the universe. I've learned
it's bats that pull the darkness into night—
a magician's trick—keep your eye on the moon.
*Hoo.* The wind is made of air, but
picks up cows, demolishes houses. The world
churns below them. The strength of the ant
is like that of the wind—Nature's little joke—
its purpose to confuse. Oh,
you gullible ones, beware—
like smoke to fire,
wind is to rain.

   **Second Coming**
Please,
give me a forbidden opportunity.
I am a fat sadness playing
nose music to the trees. It won't quit raining.
Hasn't stopped in days. Everything
is spongy. A small patch of blue appears
on the horizon, but disappears
as abruptly. The grass is a lake
of ripples. Horses, spooked
by wind, blow to the back pasture.
Rabbits, their ears billowed by gales,
spill chaotic through the fields, then float
in their burrows. Brooks are swollen
with greed for land.

Fish are leaping and buoyant,
hoping, this time,
for dominion.

### *There is No Seven*
The blink. The blank. Here
there is nothing. A day
of rest. Nothing left.
The creation. Your mind.
Then space.

## Frogs of the Evening

A raincoat drips in the hallway
while steam gathers in the kitchen.
The brightest tomatoes

are lined up on the windowsill,
ready for parboiling, and
putting-up into Mason jars.

Children are hollering
and running through the house,
while the woman's elbows bend

to the quiet rhythm of her work.
The frogs at dusk groan deeply
this time of the year.

They discuss the mystery
of winter mud, and the slow
emergence of renewal.

## The Tenor

I'm listening for the owl
to sing again. To hear
the empty holes hooting

in darkness. I'm awake, and
on a ludicrous pre-dawn walk.
In the dim light, it feels

like someone follows me.
I don't know who. An owl's
talons twist together

like Grandma's hands at prayer.
The bracken ferns rise up to whisper,
*Please bow your head with us now.*

Stone-gray mist. Bright wind.
Whose tree do I stand beneath?
Who is it that sings for me?

I've lived here like a great owl
who makes no noise in passing
in anticipation of the darkening song.

## First Frost

Last night, frost
hit the squash leaves
and began
the autumn melt.

The fledgling squashes
have little time left.

Tomatoes—once
the ice comes—
forget about them.
They've been eager
for the earth since
their hard, round
seeds sprouted from
the dirt last spring.

All summer,
their leaves curled
around, and pointed
to the ground.

But the zucchini
are a different sort,
always reaching skyward

as though in praise
of all that's worthy.

**Dear Elephant,**

My friend tells me
that, powerful as you can be,
you are afraid of mice.
I understand.

Mice have sharp little teeth.
Their eyes have no irises. Their legs
run their bellies along the ground.
They are quick as snakes. They live
underground where things decay.

You fear them because
of your ignorance. A duck
does not fear the slug,
because it pays attention
to slugs. Sure, ducks can fly,
but they know the value
of the waddle.

I understand the world
of mice. Rodents are a lot like you.
They are dark. They love to eat. They keep
ugly little tails on their backsides. But here
is a secret: You, sweet pachyderm,
can follow mice without being noticed
because you are the size of a wall.

Be brave. Mice are not sweet,
and may be just a little salty. If you lean
in close, their songs could make you cry,
so fine a tone, like a womb
thing beginning. Or the tip
of a tusk.

## About Writing Political Poetry

I don't write political poetry
because words on a page become trite,
because there is a value to life
I cannot put into words,
because I am a simpleton.

I don't write political poetry
about liars, or traitors, or patriots.
I don't write about the bias
of the electoral college, or about
how corporations are now people, or how
recent trade wars might adversely affect
our lower and middle classes.

I haven't written about our president,
or how this one applauds dictators,
shakes hands with tyrants, congratulates
human rights abusers.

I don't write political poetry
because my words disappear
in the wind, because even though
marching and chanting, the rattling
of signs, and the shaking of fists
have happened, the tyranny continues.
I am helpless and too stupid
to make the slightest difference.

I haven't written political poems
because I am footless within history,
have no leg to stand on, and believe
that having no knowledge of a heritage
has created the vast majority of angry
white non-people who demand

to be real without an understanding
of just who they might be. Let's
take a breath here.

I would like to write political poetry.
There are people coming to America.
Right now, they are knocking
at our borders. They are desperate
and dirty. Their feet are blistered.
They desire a safe place, a small haven
to wash up, and to eat a decent meal
without fear. But we've shut the door,
locked it, built higher, longer, and
sharper walls to keep them away.
We've threatened these travelers
with soldiers, taken their children,
cursed and spat at them, sprayed
tear gas on them—as though
they haven't cried enough—
and insist they walk through a pinhole
to gain the refuge they need.

Our country is beautiful,
but it is angry.
Our country is spacious,
but we are stingy.
*My country, 'tis of thee.*
*Let all that breathe partake.*
I don't write political poetry
because I don't know where
to start, and wouldn't know
where to stop.

**Dear Gerald Stern,**

Last night, I dreamt
I was a chicken.
A little Cornish
game. What a life!
What a lift! It was like
sitting in the window
of a sail, the telltales
pointing to future truths.
When I awoke, I thought,
*Soaring with eagles is*
*overrated.*

A hen is well grounded.
That's a fact.

Now—fully awake—I do realize
that I am not a chicken.
But perhaps I am not unlike the fowl
scattered and picking under my table,
near the dogs. Especially the ones
who choose the smallest
of crumbs, as in the old
masters' paintings. The whole affair
appears as a tasty dinner, even
the divine scent of cigar
trailing after. You and I
both know the beauty of that:
the mesmerizing smoke
rising like priority ghosts,
the insignificant ashes
tumbling to the tile.

So, dear Mr. Stern,
now that we're older,

I have some questions
for you. Have you ever played
cribbage in a chicken coop?
Have you ever unearthed
an egg from the ear of a child?
When was the last time
you were the possum? Would
you haggle with life all over again?
That is the question. I know you're
tired now. Everyone is. Give up
your answer when you can.
I'll be setting on the roost
in the saddle of the storm,
ready and waiting, like always.

## Song of the Liar

The weatherman says it is sixty-six
degrees outdoors on this mid-morning,
mid-week, mid-summer day. Ennui
is the jello flavor of the month.

The thermometer reads seventy-five,
the weatherman has met his sweltering point—
another torpid detail of the day.
This is naturally a political argument.

The first riff of Stravinsky's *Firebird*
burbles in the air. Truth is the composer
ate seeds for breakfast. He is still hungry.
The day is falsified with the twitting

of birds who once sang arias with glee.
The Indian plum's ripe fruit has blackened,
and teems with the humming of bees.
Our president is dreadful.

Just thought I'd mention it.
We fill our minds these days
with the slow beating of bass drums
as though they are cellos,

as though music was meant
as a backdrop for this discord of sobs.
A measured precision never stops
pummeling the supposed harmonic tones.

The red-eyed fly the color of damage—
the one who's landed in this journal
beside my loaded pen—is also a liar.
The lacerated grass has never

smelled this spicy before, pungent
as an argument, but far more relaxing.
I can hear the sounds of the stars
gritting through space. I can hear

the dancing of the celestial bodies,
the rustling of silks, the beads rattling,
bells ringing. The liar sings louder
and louder into the red-hot silence.

## Lost Shadow

A long time ago to me, but not to the earth,
when many people lived where many more do now,
all the women wore dresses, and men combed
their hair back. The horses were round and beautiful.

A cold, easy breeze drifts through the early dawn
as I carry an armful of hay for the black and grey horses
who clump and nudge, following close behind.
Their steamy breath blows silently, and warms my neck.

Back then, I had a true friend. My partner and I rode
those horses, spirited and laughing, to the top of every
winding logging road in the foothills, daring steep sides
and fast curves. But one dark, condensated night,

he fell into a ditch so deep he never came out again,
and the nightmare began, the flashing of blues and reds.
He was lost from the earth, the horses calling for days,
but no answer. Even today, riding the darkest horse,

I sometimes catch a glimpse of him rounding the bend
ahead, disappearing into the thickest fog. When I follow,
pushing the horse for more, I never catch up, but keep on
cantering anyway, just in case, until there's nowhere to go.

## An Abridged Year, Condensed

Last February, the rains
soaked the ground until the fields
shivered like jello. Wood ducks stormed
the pond, whistling down
like little bombs. Nothing happened.

The rains continued through March,
each day the water table seduced
the earth. Our bickering tasted of pond scum.
A drenched cottontail dashed across the road,
and dove with a splash into the underbrush.

When the rain finally let up: drizzle.
April overflowed with questions
of fog, of god, and the mist that stands
in ditches like angels. My bones
drink the air as though I'm alive again.

The entire month of May happened like this:
the blossoms choked themselves
out of the murky loam, we settled back
into the green lines that rose
selflessly from the earth. The worms,
both red and white, warmed
our backsides and innards. That's all.

If June and July didn't become August,
I have no idea where they went. Time
passed by like it had always been history,
the book standing musty on the shelf. Hot sun
diminished by cold-blooded clouds, it
wasn't difficult to sit beside the fire.
By this time, the neighbor's roosters

already lost their heads. Not a surprising detail.
Stew pots are made for comfort.

When September trickled onto the landscape,
we both awakened to the sudden warmth
of the sun. A blue dot rolled across our inner eyelids,
dragging a red screen behind. An entertainment.
Cats sprawled across the lawn. This time, no birds.

I love October: the way the leaves
run from their mother trees; the deathly
chill in the morning air; those bird
suicides under the windows. I have
to love this month. Otherwise.

November scares the pants off me. It's
the wickedest month of the year. A pair
of feral dogs run onto the porch: they
glare into the living room and show their prickly teeth,
broadcasting an ugly growl. It's been an odd year.

Our holiday dinner, begun in November,
finishes by the end of December. Takes awhile,
being only the two of us now. The noisy Canada geese
fly at 45 miles per hour, no tail wind. Their Vs point
everywhere but south. They zig-zag overhead.
I don't know what that means. I am lost.

At the beginning of the year, something changes.
The air. What was blue turns scarlet, or yellow.
The aroma of decay acquires a heady spice,
and you and I breathe it in like relief. Grinning.
Expectations arrive! What is it about a new year?

## Five Fields

Kindling.

Under dim winter light,
trees stand naked. The one there
is dying from the inside out.

Ablaze.

Fire excites poets.
To confirm this idea, burn
the little books they publish.

Nocturne.

Two old horses stand
beside tall cedars and wait.
Soon, the rain will stop.

Stalemate.

When a man knows
he'll be hanged in a fortnight,
what does he think of?

Flight.

The dog up the road
has barked for days on end.
Sing, little bird, sing.

## Mosquitoes
*after Lucia Perillo*

Like the dragonfly, we dart, and dodge,
and also slap at the mosquito, who places
itchy red welts on our limbs.
Buzzing in our ears, they bite
our ankles. It's the females who dive
for our blood. The males are meek,
and just want to have sex. Any bare-skinned,
hoping-to-be-tan-soon person can
unwittingly be bitten and sucked dry.
Red welts instead of roses at the prom,
though bug spray fills our lungs.

I am spotted as a polka-dot dress,
a leopard, the nine of dominoes.
The nippers are nowhere to be seen.
How do I explain the acne-like bumps
on my face? Too much chocolate?
What about those red rolling hills
on my arms? A benign case of smallpox?

The problem is access, as if our skin
were large as a red and white tablecloth;
or the Great Plains; as though a tiger sucks
blood through its nose. The mosquito is
a professional pilot that has been crossed
with a nurse who is conscious only
of your veins. From six feet away, the mosquito
can perform a six-point landing on the exact vein
with the correct flow and pressure necessary
for a quick dip and a speedier take-off.

Though they may thrum in your ears,
they partake and leave silently as burglars.

First, they are here, pestering incessantly.
Then, nothing.
Except for the red lumps left behind.
How can they be so present, and then—
*poof*—gone, disappeared, dissolved into thin air?
While we sit and wonder where they go,

they'll dip their beaks into the other arm,
and gratefully sip as though of milk and honey.

## If You Must Crow, Unsew Your Mouth, Open Wide, and Let the Flies Begin

### *Barking Cats*
Exactly like the brassy crowing hen,
and the booted whistling girl, one
can be much more successful
than predicted. A fate of virtue
needs only a draft of warm air,
and a good pair of wings.
Sometimes, a cat will bark like a dog.
Sometimes, it hacks up a hairball.
Perhaps the extraordinary
is actually the ordinary.

### *Carrying On*
An ant can carry
a massive amount of weight
for it's size—twenty times
or more. But is surpassed by
the dung beetle. There are frogs
who jump so high, a person
would need to leap 38 stories to compare.
The frog would care more about the ant
and the dung beetle. Still,
even the tiny flea can hop higher
than a frog.

### *If I Could Crow*
It's been proven that
one dysfunctional ovary, and,
poof, you're a rooster.
Before that can happen,
one must be a hen.

### The Miraculous and the Divine
The mongoose and
the cobra is an old story.
Speed and cunning,
poison and awe.
We won't even discuss
the Christ Lizard.

### The Insomniac
Under the warm lights or
in the bubbling darkness
of an aquarium, the zebra-fish
are insomniacs. They cannot
relax enough to hover in place,
nor think of using a pillow. They may
be afraid of the dark.
They may need the security
of an ultraviolet night light,
something that can glow in the dark,
like a scorpion.

### Bragging Rights
If you could shoot
blood from your eye
like the horned lizard,
would you brag about it? And how!

### Are You Ticklish?
The polite answer is "No."
A rat loves to laugh;
is so ticklish it will
finish a maze faster
for a quick tickling
than for a tasty treat.
Perhaps laughter is the sound geese make
as they head south to warmer climes

during a blustery pre-winter storm,
and again as they hurry back north again,
looking for Spring's promise of a good time.
Do you think this is true?
The polite answer is "No."

## Existential Pastoral

How can you not look at the stars,
as each drags a path of light
around the earth? They follow
a trajectory I understand,
but my vocabulary can't pinpoint
their origin and final fading labors,
nor the significant distance between us.

My ignorance is confined to words
from the mouth and hand, the darkness
of ink, a deafness of comprehension.

My old mare has wandered blindly
around the pastures for years.
She follows meandering trails
she created years ago, and eats the bird song
of grasses that taste like spring. Darkness
is a comforting companion
for her fading eyes.

She could translate this unimaginable
pleasantness of stars and song
into terms I might comprehend,
but there's a barrier we can't pass.

So, I'll try again
with another scenario closer to home.
The homeless woman on the corner,
the scruffy man beside his bags—
they appear randomly desperate,
and look straight into my eyes.
I look away to see whatever else
can occupy my vision. Are they
offering me a chance to be kind?

They may approach me any day,
but stand back instead, waiting
like old fence posts toppling ever so slowly,
a welcome sign—handwritten—
in their hands, as they travel
the paths they've made.

Like a rabbit in the garden,
my whiskers tremble as I
do damage I don't understand,
and eat my fill of everything,
aware only of my fears.

## Earnestly Banished

> *"You are an expatriate, see?*
> *You hang around cafés."*
> —Ernest Hemingway, The Sun Also Rises

The last time you lost,
not in the fisticuffs of love,
but in the scuttling of intent,
you were set out on the corner
between the scrap cans and bins.

You had gotten so precious
for a while, glittery as moonlit frost,
until you took on the tiresome tinge
of the exile. The fake standards you follow
have brought only ruin. Why don't you drink

yourself to death while you're at it?
You are obsessed with obsessions
and the side effects of your prescriptions.
You spend all your time chattering, unemployed,
nonfunctional, and too well known.

You've lost touch with the soil,
old man of the puddle—the very dirt
that would have been your savior
had you savored even a gritty spoonful
lightly salted across your tongue.

Your door is unhinged. The stew is overdone.
The fire has calmed to embers.
Lights are going out all over America.
Your creaky rocker is dusty with soot and snooze.
Isn't it time you wandered back home?

## Sitting Like Clowns

in a pair of club chairs,
a geneticist and his basset
were deep in conversation.

As daylight chased the horizon,
the two simultaneously
ate ice-cream, and discussed

the revisions in DNA, seawater,
and the effects of repetitive actions.
The dog barely said a word

until after the last sip was gone.
Under a heavily burled brow,
the dog finally uttered, "Life needs

no tears; Oceans give no apologies.
We're here in this life simply
for relaxation. Not one
will get out alive."

## Meat and Potatoes

I am not in favor of the potato.
The potato was once the treasure
of the faithful farmers of Ireland.
Generations of the Irish nurtured
and cultivated the ill-willed potato,
and still, the notorious spud turned
on the Irish. I call for an abolishment
of those hard-headed beasts
with their multiple buggy eyes.
Those bog apples!

I am, however, in favor of beef.
Cows exist on earth. It's a simple fact.
But the reason is not completely
evolutionary. Bovines have crept
into every capitalist's dream
to the point that, if it weren't
for the meat-eaters' hearty appetites,
beef cows would become extinct.
They must be placed part and parcel
in little white trays at the grocers.
Put out to pasture on their own,
cattle can't care for themselves.
They are not cuddly as kittens.
Their maintenance is expensive
and they have a stench.
In a purely vegetarian world,
no one would buy beef. Cows
would not go to market, thereby
creating their demise. Life,
being sacred, means that we must assist
the cows. Strangely then, in order to live,
a cow must be eaten. If the beef needs a side
of potato, so be it. A ladle of gravy
in this life is not too much to ask.

## What Tasted Bad Then and Still Does Today

Liver
Lima beans
Canned peas
Canned green beans
Canned corn
Canned spinach
Kidneys
Bread pudding
Breaded meatloaf
Hash browns (using half bread, half potatoes)
Canned raviolis
Canned tomato soup
The tongue swell of Krusteaz pancake mix
Miracle Whip
American Cheese
Pickles, especially sweet
Squash, yams and sweet potatoes
when cooked with brown sugar
Aspic with green olives and pimento
Any berry except the huckle on a hike

See? There isn't all that much.

Most can go down
quick as a pill
with a big gulp of milk.

Kidneys and liver
make nice little treats
for the dog
the cat
the vacuum cleaner.

A paper napkin
wadded just so
can disguise
a decent-sized ball
of canned anything.

A small handful
of whatever's left
can find its way down
the white gullet of a toilet.

A word for the brave child—
hold tight with all your might.
Eat like a monster,
growling and glaring.

A word for the miserable child—
stare and stare at your so-called food.
Suddenly, it will become
a foreign landscape
for you alone to explore.
May this be your first
lesson in artistry.

A word to the stubborn child—
if all else fails
sit there weeping quietly
for hours until
everyone else
falls asleep.

Remember there isn't
much you don't like.
Never forget.

*The Importance of Average Miracles*

## The Importance of Average Miracles

I've seen the inside of a chicken
and walked away amazed.

If you're hungry, the best
are white Cornish Crosses, Jersey
Black Giants, or that mean one-eyed
Barred Rock rooster that's taken up the habit
of spurring anyone within eye-shot.
But any old hen will do
if you own a good-sized stew pot.

Poultry must be killed in just the right way.
With none of that running around the yard
like the infamous chicken. If you've never
seen it done, read a book. You'll learn
the best method is to stick a chicken
in the brain with the sharp end of a knife.
Disgusting, yet effective, like the solution
to most obstacles in life. Do it
as directed and the chicken
will be nonplussed, the meat
tender as possible. Then the throat
must be slit so all bleeds out. Be heedful.
It is important that the sticky red syrup
drain as completely as that of the oil
when maintaining a car, but
more tenderly and empathetic.

But before you even begin,
it is essential to calm the chicken.
For the tenderest meat, be sure
the young chicken is not tense. Help it
to relax. Hold it in your lap,
stroke its head and neck.

Don't be in a hurry. Then
kill it, as above. This action will also
enable you to feel better, knowing
the chicken found peace before it left.

Feather plucking is simple
once you've dunked the bird upside down
into a pot of boiling hot water. Put it in,
swirl, and take it out again. Then the feathers
can be plucked by the handful, and stuffed
into a sack to dry. A pillow stuffing bonus.

You've gotten this far.
Let's examine the purpose of a chicken,
as possibly established in Eden. Begin by drawing
a line with your sharp knife from the point
of the chicken's lower breast to its anus. Careful there.
Cut clean and cautious around the circumference
of the anus. Open the chicken and behold!
Take some time to look around, for inside
resides a miracle. There is order where your imagination
runs wild with green guts and ooze, slime and chaos.
Entropy does not exist inside the chicken. Everything
is meticulously clean. One thing leads to another,
all engineered with purpose and efficiency.
Nothing is wasted. Even the fat that pads the belly
protects the delicacy of shell better than bubble-wrap
ever could. Filth is encased in a flexible tubing
mindfully engineered just for that purpose.

Eggs!—the most miraculous part of the chicken.
Notice the entire lack of shell particles in there.
None are present. In the productive hen,
the small globes of yolk, bright and golden,
are arranged in such a way that each future
egg precedes another until they become

microscopic, a spiraling nebula,
a minuscule universe. It's like an ancient calendar,
a strange measuring device, a helix
of tiny suns inside the body of a hen.

The miracle of chickenhood is not finished yet—
because the egg is a hand-held miracle. Take another
peek inside. Do you see the conveyor belt
where eggs become covered in shell? No?
And how, exactly, do they stay so clean,
inside and out, when they move through
the same tube designed for the daily delivery

of filthy pre-aged fertilizer? Don't think
too long on that one. Once transported
to the nest, the ovoid egg is perfectly devoid
of grime. Egg collection should be often,
lest the chicken sit too long atop the egg and
have an accident, or on a rainy day, a muddy foot
might sully the shell.

The immaculate chicken's egg
—an everyday miracle—
is one of the original wonders of the world.

## The Egg is a Damsel

The Egg is a Damsel.
When she wakes, she picks up her needle
and begins. Blue
is a thread of sunlight today.

The Dog licks her nose,
then sneezes into a shaft
of dawn. She sings
in praise of dust motes.

The Bird is a Fly
with a bottle on her back.
Blue as inner ice, and more
melancholy.

The Horse is old.
Her legs—thin lines
penciled to the ground.
Water drips from her lips.

The Barn holds a Cat
and an Opossum. Because the Mice
have left, these two avoid
the other's gaze.

The Day has fallen
to its knees, begging
forgiveness
from these particular creatures.

**Buttercups**

When the flowers of buttercups
drop their yellow petals,
there is an orb left behind
with sharp points that catch
on your socks as you pass—
hitchhikers intent on traveling
to set down roots elsewhere.

This plant offers a way to learn
whether you like butter, or not.
No need to take a taste,
just the reflection
of a single buttercup
flashing under your chin
will tell you the answer.

There is an Italian chicken
called the Sicilian Buttercup
that have two red combs
on their heads running
side by each, front to back.
Perhaps they like butter, too,
with a little sage and garlic.

## Why Roosters Are Odious

In the first rays of day,
the rooster stirs, restless.
He grumbles a bit about
the slow rise of the sun
before he begins to crow.
The rooster is angry all day
because he never calls
as loudly as he wishes, and
he knows the answers to nothing,
except where the best bits of grubs
are kept, and which is the finest
of the hens, and why.

But at night, late, the rooster begins
to dream he is Gullinkambi,
the golden-combed rooster the height
of a horse who roams the Old Norse mountains.
The rooster has dreamt of the unceasing
crescendo of Gullinkambi's roar
ringing in the final days of the earth.
He knows Gullinkambi could tell
whatever you want to know,
and a lot more. He knows which wolf
swallowed Odin, and who stole
what horse and when.

When morning comes again,
the rooster mutters and moans
as the day brightens. Though he
hones his spurs, and performs
a stompy dance, his stature
is in his dreams. When he steps
into the sun, he will crow every day
as loud as he can, forever disappointed.

## Why a Chicken Lays an Egg

A hen has a calendar.
On it is a list of the days
she will lay an egg.

This is the reason she lives for.
Each Nebula of Yolk is a star.
A star for every day marked
on her calendar.

Oh, there's the crow of the rooster,
too. He is so optimistic. And the bits
of insect and leaf he points out!
Looky here, he says.
But that is secondary to the egg,
in the hen's mind.

Each egg is marked on her calendar
because there is nothing in her life
more important. That is why
they are packaged so carefully—
first the albumen, a special concoction
of mystery and yum, and then
the swift and fragile production
of the hard-cover book filled
with the knowledge of being.
She knows each egg
means a safe landing
for another star on this earth.

That is why each day at dawn,
or perhaps later in the afternoon,
she is beyond elation as a warm
three-dimensional oval plops

neatly and clean onto the straw
beneath her tail feathers.

Be-gawk! Amen!
And why the heck not?

## When a One-Eyed Sphinx Moth Lays an Egg

She doesn't stop at just the one. She lays hundreds
of little white pearls, one after the other, in piles here

and there. Color-coded, the eggs turn green
and donut-shaped just before they hatch.

Once loosed from the shell, they are tiny lime-green
caterpillars less than half an inch long.

This particular moth devours willow leaves
like candy. Their tiny heads move up and down

the leaf as it disappears, bit by bit, down their gullets.
From there, the growth spurt begins and never ends

until one day, after half a tree's worth of willow leaves
have disappeared, it stops. Then the caterpillar

climbs out of itself, abandons the husk of 'pillar
like an old fur coat dropped in front of the new changeling.

Now, there is a rotund, shortened version of the cat'
that squirms and wriggles like Jabba the Hutt,

changing color in circles first, from bright green
to amber, and finally all at once to chocolate brown.

That is the chrysalis laying there under the dirt. What
was green and chomping will now sleep through winter

and then emerge next summer as a large moth
with scalloped wings who will never eat a thing.

## Pastoral: Late August, Mid-Morning

A pair of old horses
browse the bony forest.

Fog murks through brambles,
prickles the horses' backs.

They stand, still
as the trees, their legs
a confusion of underbrush.

## The Impact of Beauty

Things are always changing.
One day is beautiful.
Quiet. Snow feathering
across the fields. Clear ice
thickly coating the black branches.

She takes the brown horse out
of the gloomy barn into the bright
gray of the day. They stop.
He stands there: head up, nostrils
flared, swishing his black tail, snorting.
The world is mismatched from yesterday,
and it sets him on edge.

They walk into the cold, slow wind.
Snow burdens the trees. Ice
constricts their movement.
Cottonwoods shiver and snap.
Here and there, clumps of branches
tumble to the ground. Everything
is falling. Even the horse, nearer
the pond, lays down and rolls.
Snow sticks to his body.
He gets up with a kick.

What comes next
is fine to see—the beauty
of a horse—all that prancing,
the head proud. A dance
between horse and landscape.
She lets him go for a while.

When she collects him, she's wary,
holds him on a loose line and stays
away. Never trust a nervous horse, they say.

This is her closing memory:
he walks beside her in the snowy field,
watching her, listening to the babel
that follows wind. The pond groans.

A fault splits along its perimeter.
The horse swings his head sideways,
quick and crazy, a swat at the fly
called her head. Suddenly, she is curled
on a bed of snow. Suddenly, she is asleep.
She dreams of the magnificent beauty
of red roses in snow. The horse
stands beside her, silent
in the new darkness of her day.

### The Bearer of Light and Dark
*for my Appaloosa, Moby (at 30)*

My gray mare is sometimes dappled;
sometimes white with dots of black
and brown showing up
and disappearing like
the sun's loving freckles.

She fiddles on long, black legs,
balances the tip of one back foot
onto the earth just so.
There are dark cracks within her
white-striped hooves. They won't
go away. She is old, and this
is how the end begins. Small parts
leave slowly. With the left eye gone
now, she has only the right—
the one eye and the blank socket.
How she stumbles, heedless,
in her dark days.

The curved plum of her eye turns
away from deep browns
toward the light. A dusty
white sheen draws across the top,
which sets neatly into a swollen puff
of the surrounding lids.
At times, her eyelid glistens,
inked with the greasiness
of healing ointments. Her lashes
flutter, and clench, flutter,
like bees on a flower.
And then—the eye, shining,
appears between the thick shade of her lid.

For years, she stood waiting
for her daily doses: a quick
poke in the eye, twice, two times a day.

She'll wait in the sun.
She'll wait in the rain.
She waits for the flies
to freeze. Waits while
the grass grows green. Patient,
she listens to every sound
that has ever happened
in her field, seeing more
than could possibly be in range.

There are those who say white
is not a color. They are
the same ones who say black
is a collection of all colors—
a beautiful thought.

The ghost of my horse
will be white. The ghost
of my horse will
also be black. She will never
be running, but circling
alone in her grayness—the one
possession she owns—
a gift from the fog
of over 10,000 dusks and dawns.
When she leaves

this place, she will still
be here. I know this,
because truth has a way
of showing itself,
no matter how doubtful.

## Questioning the Immortality of Horses

After seeing how she went down,
how she squeezed her eyes shut,
how she lay there breathing hard
under a hot and ignorant sun,
how her nostrils flared,
how her teeth showed between her lips,
how she labored to get up,
though her legs would buckle,
and she would topple,
and the dust would rise,

after running to get her halter,
after her nose lifted to receive it,
after experiencing the relief of the fastened clasp,
then following her efforts to rise,
after straining to heft this weight from the dirt,
and accepting the scorch of the rope on the palm
after seeing her strength surrender,
after feeling her drop, the force of her,
after staring into the stupid sun,
after attempting to give her some shade,
after the gesture of feeding her a small carrot,
her eye open and round as her lips reached for it,
after forty-five minutes
when she rose again,

after thinking about the alternatives,
about what if she didn't get up, and then
about what would happen if she collapsed
in her stall, or slipped in the mud,
if she went down in the woods,
if she went down beyond the pond,

if she went down in the pond,
After struggling with preserving
the spirit of life, the simple worthiness of it,
after laboring with the idea of pain,
after speculation about existence and the ancient,
after contemplating history and our future,
and the duration of all of it,
after seeing her down
with her eyes wincing,
the question persists.

### Like Wings

*This poem is in a Golden Shovel form, with the ends
words in each line formed from a line in "Juan's Song"
by Louise Bogan.*

The autumn of the tundra—when
swans raise their white wings, beauty
rises to bleak grey skies. The weakened sun breaks

across the lake, brilliant for an instant, and
then forgotten sudden as a dream. A golden leaf falls
from the aspens—a leader whose disciples are torn asunder
from the trees by the next few gusts. This year, I

am the round-eyed horse in the ice storm. He knows to feel
the ground with each step. He has the nerve, but no
spirit to serve the frozen ground. His trot carries the grief

of the future, while crazed frost thickens across his back. For
though the earth carries the wide wings of swans, it
drops thunder across the lake of ice. The horse slips and all but
falls in the darkness, yet he is filled, as always, with wonder.

## The Orchard

Whenever I finish
eating an apple,
I think of my horse.

The dark one
with a spirit of storm
rumbling daily.

I would give
this core to her
if she were here.

But she is not
anymore. The sky
is blue today,

and the core
is turning brown
in the compost.

Whenever I finish
an apple, a pear, an ear of corn,
I look out toward the field,

and see how long
the grass has grown,
now she's gone.

The rabbits and finches,
horsetails and thistles,
have also returned.

Whenever I leave
this life, it would be
more than enough

to be planted as
a feral apple seed,
and offer red or golden fruits

to the passing deer
and rabbits.
The horses.

# The Forceps Baby

My parents were quite normal, but
I was born a mutilated forceps baby.
My right eye swollen shut, bruised
as a beaten housewife's. My bald head,
scraped and welted by the tongs,
carries a spot that never grew hair.

"Ugliest baby I ever saw,"
they laughed.

When I dream, I've learned never
to grab hold of anything that might move.
Pick up the end of a dog's leash,
and the words "Run, Spot, run,"
rush through my mind. The dog
at the other end of the leash rises,
and tears off. She could be chasing
anything. And I am pulled along
squalling like a baby. The dog
cracks the tail end of the leash
like a whip. Baby-me is flapping
at the end, as in a hurricane gale,
but cannot let go. The dog pulls harder,
runs faster. If baby-me lets go now,
I might not survive the freedom. My sudden
white dress would be ruined.

I wake from my dreams gasping for air
from a claustrophobic passageway.
No sense in crying about it.
Back then, I learned a forceps baby
will be pulled through the channel of life
always at the wrong end of the tongs.

## Summary of Our Childhood
*for my four brothers*

We were angels.
We got into a lot of trouble.

Though we were good.
Though we were quiet.

We were angels.
But we were pretty stupid.

Though we knew better.
Though we were practical.

We were such angels.
We could sing.

We could play music.
Though we were unclean.

Though others called us names.
We were truly angels.

Though we daydreamed on the long hard pews.
Though we passed notes.

Though we were sweaty.
Though we were alarmed and afraid.

We wrestled with each other.
We threw things at each other.

Though we were spanked,
and whipped, and scolded,

we were golden. We
were just like angels.

## The Line-Up

  The gray rain and the grayer clouds
of early spring. My mother alone
in the house with my four brothers and me.
Each of us young, and sweaty with lethargy.

  The rain pounds the porch. We are standing
in the pea green living room. There is a large furnace-
grate on the floor just inside the hallway to our right
that sometimes burns grids onto the soles of our feet.

  It is almost six o'clock now. Our mother has lined
us up with our backs to the wall beside the hall. She
is rumbling thunder. She has a wooden spoon in hand.
Our father will come home soon and remove his belt.

  We will become an entire children's choir
howling out our songs. These are the lessons
we will learn: We are stupid. We are evil.
We are sinners. God loves us. We will be punished.

  The gray rain and the grayer clouds
of early spring. My mother alone in the house
with my four brothers and me. Each of us
young and sweaty and unloved, except,
perhaps, by God.

## Ode to My Unpresent Tonsils

I've missed you over the years,
dear tonsils. Not because you left me
at the early age of five, nor because you caused
the second worst nightmare of my life:
the head of an angry-faced clown suspended
from a horizontal string strung through the ears
and bobbing in front of a moldery hospital-green wall;
the raging head doggedly spewed a stream inspired
only by the ungodly. And I was
just a little kid! Nor do I wish you gone
for the scoops of ice cream I was served
upon your abrupt absence, nor the jello,
not even for my newfound love of junket.

While the word "tonsillectomy"
does not leave me unamused—a pinball
of a word that rolls around one's mouth
hitting this, missing that, and coming
back home to "me"—this is not
why I miss you.

You once dangled brightly in the back row
of my mouth, unnoticed until you swelled up
unwitting as a pair of bright red hot-air balloons,
an unpleasant set of seething bulbous balls
back there, and yet you were thought to be evolution's
obsolete organ. But you were not
completely useless.

Before you left, I thought I'd swallowed a honeybee,
and you, like some sort of throat-goalie,
caught that bee before it dove into the net of my lungs.
But this idea soon appeared unmistakably untrue. Even though

you unfurled an excess of white blood cells and antibodies
to protect me from harm, your performance is not missed
as much as you might think.

In fact, the only time I truly miss the two of you is when
another person asks, "Do you still have your tonsils?"
When I have to tell them "No," I suddenly find myself
looking into the far reaches of the mouths of whoever
happens to still have theirs. That is when I miss you most.
For if you hadn't cut out of my life so soon
I would be answering that question with my mouth
open wide to proudly share the vision of you,
my twin darlings, to whoever asked to meet you.

## When Thorns of the Hawthorn Pierce the Soul

When you prick your finger
on the spiny branches of the Hawthorn,
do you bleed? Do you cry out?
Do you know what you whine about?
Isn't your wish for eternal life possibly
over-rated? Have you asked yourself
whose thoughts could be that
fascinating forever? How long
will the Hawthorn reach out for you?
Why do you look away from me?

Why put your fingers in your ears,
wipe the cobwebs from your hair, scrape
the dirt from your nails? Are those bees
buzzing in your mouth? Why do you
stand in the field surrounded by six-foot tall
canary grass, peeking through the blades
to stare up at that one wisp of a cloud up there?
Why do you tremble so?

Is your soul a raggedy bag of bones?
Is it fulfilling enough to look longingly
toward the sad blue sky and hum
once in a while? Will your life spill open
one day like a ball of baby spiders
flung into the wind? To risk your life
is one thing, but why cut down
the entire bloody tree? Its branches
flower white over your head fully laden
with the sound of honey bees, but do the thorns
point to your throat? Will the wild
red berries poison you?

Is this your shoddy
notion of rapture: the omission
of pain? Did you truly expect the streets
of gold? The gates studded with pearls?
What a useless idea to nurture the soul!
How can you gather the truth
when you haven't the foggiest
sense of eternity? Didn't our genius creator
give us linear time just so we'd know
death, though his endless timeline
resides among us? Do you wonder
what that even means?

## Chewing Gum, a Pity

It's surprising,
isn't it? When
the memories
come gushing.

Shoelace
chewing gum!
I'd completely
forgotten!
And then,
wham. Someone
mentioned it
with disgust
and sorrow.

Suddenly there
it was—
the dirty taste
in the mouth
of sweaty cotton
and gritty dirt.

I remember.
I don't know
why I remember.
But I do.

The wet
wet shoelace
filling up with saliva
while being chewed,
and chewed
and chewed.

This particular flavor
and texture. Not bad,
actually. Only thing missing
is the bubbles. You simply
cannot make bubbles
with shoelaces.
Such a pity.

**Growing Pains**

Playground 1963. Mark Holsather twirled me around and
   around and around in the covered playground just
   outside the rain. We were laughing and laughing—until
   I ran into a metal post and received the second biggest
   black eye of my life.
In the early '70's, I used to stay over at Margie's place,
   listening to rock and roll at high volume, smoking a bit of
   dope, we would sing and laugh louder than the music. Her
   parents were old, and hard of hearing.
Back in '77, the first kiss from the man I would marry landed on
   my lips. His neck smelled exactly like the garden of Eden.
On the playground of 1962, Mark Holsather, the neighbor
   from up the road, was accused of being my boyfriend. We
   swore we were just were friends. No kissing. No marriage.
   No babies. Only a tree to climb for the view.
All my life, I never wore lipstick, other than the Avon samples
   some snarky friend handed me one fine day.
Just out of high school in '73, I was hired to drive a school bus
   route between Mount Lake Terrace and Everett. Half the
   kids were taller than me and just as sassy.
In '75, my best friend in high school dated, became pregnant,
   and married a man who just got out of prison, lived in a
   half-way house, and spit snoose in cups left in surprising
   places all over the house. I could never find her again.
During the early '90's, I bought a green Appaloosa. I read a
   book to learn how to break her. She was eager to learn.
   One day, that horse taught me how to fly. I saw the shiny
   top of the barn roof, a bird's eye view of the pasture
   below, and took a crash course in how to land. I was a
   fast learner. Gave myself a B-minus and a headache that
   lasted for weeks.
During my childhood, I wore neighborhood hand-me-downs.
   My favorite was the fluorescent green, pink, and black
   striped dress. Four boys would follow me around the

junior high halls saying nasty things I can't repeat. The dress still burns in memory.

All of February 2017, the biggest black eye of my life developed like a kaleidoscope, as did my perspective of the world.

On a foggy night in '74, a cop pulled up behind my '47 Chevrolet named Otis parked alongside the roadway. The windows were steamy. My boyfriend stepped out of the car and gesticulated apologies to the man. I wasn't wearing lipstick.

During my mid-20's in the early '80's, Barry and I lived on 20 acres along with three cats, two dogs, chickens with names like Tricky Woo, Cedric and Henrietta, Samson and Delila; plus Blossom the milk goat; sheep called Fatso, Number Two, Layla, Toots, and Small Hunk; three little pigs who assumed the names of security guards, and also a pair of ducks and Chinese geese that rounded up the herds of slugs in the garden.

2017 was an eon ago and yesterday. It was Jim who picked me out of the snow after the skinny brown horse spooked in the ice storm and whacked my head with his. I do not remember that I spit out teeth while Jim walked me to the house to clean up. I don't remember that he drove me to the ER, only that I woke up there, my sister beside me, Jim asking to go home.

## An Early Primer

At first,
I went down
and down
into the musty
dank. One stair
at a time
I went.
Not falling,

but crawling.
There I found
my mother standing
beside the light
bulb and washing
machine. She was thin
and irked. She was fat
in the middle,
and skinny.
Mostly, she
was angry.
How stupid
of me to go
where I should
not have gone.
She was burning,

and yet
she was the safe
haven in the house.
The morning's first
light. The aroma
of the coffee and
the toast. The chauffeur
of vacuum and rag.

She carried me
and the wet
laundry up
the stairs. Hung
us out to dry.
Ironed and
folded us.
Then put us
neatly away.

## Once I had a Dad

There was a time when we were afraid of our father
who wasn't in heaven: We were instructed
that his name shall be "Daddy."

When we were commanded
to stand in a row in front of him,
Mommy stood behind him,
her lips a thin line, hands on hips.
Our eyes would see the glory of our feet,
and Daddy's feet, and our feet again.
The fire was about to be lit. Things would
warm up by hand—or a belt, a big
wooden spoon, or a hairbrush—
and each of our bottoms.

We learned the act of camouflage,
how to make ourselves tiny, become invisible,
a lesson we would not forgot.

Daddy was an owl who stayed up late,
left early. To follow him would be
to follow the tiger: not too bright.
But like a bird in love, he'd
fly home again.

Our Father was the word and the word
was his. He was the protector of us
from the great and horrible holy spirit
so we shalt not die.
And on the seventh day, Daddy
would mow the lawn, flip pancakes,
drink coffee. And on the Sabbath,
he would kneel and pray, rise and sing.

Daddy was frustrated. He was anxious.
He was an angry mule.
He was a rose bush in winter:
black sticks and thorns.
We waited for the spring.

And then we flew.
And then we hated him.
And then we grew large.
And then he loved us.
And then we forgave him.
And he forgave us.
And then we rejoiced in the world.

Daddy said Yes. And he said All Right.
And Daddy did not hurt us.
And it was good.
Praise be to the forests,
and to the sticks of the forest,
and the cool green of the mosses
as they press lightly onto the big
and little bruises of our lives.

## In Another Life

Once upon a time, we had a kitten name Sylvester and a kitten named Mr. Bill who disappeared together into the dark and stormy night. The end.

Though I don't mean this, I'll say it anyway: There was a cat who was king of the house by the name of Garfield. And on the third day, he was the resurrection of the cartoon character in the funnies.

There once was a kitten named Kickens—a sickly, fragile cat—who, one day, became the most ancient feline of the house. When this delicate, elderly feline started taking on the big, rambling neighbor cats—fur tufts lolling across the turf—she became indoor-only. This is why she carried her tangle of hair all the way to twenty-one.

A long time ago, a dilute calico named Ginger kept watch on the porch. A country cat. A mouser. Lost.

At a time when I was still learning the idea of language, a kitten named Calico taught me the meanings of the words "calico," "sad," and "tire." The end. Again.

There once lived a calico named Curry. Long hair. Short legs. She was the Cheshire cat who squeezed her eyes shut to think. Opened them at each increment of thought. She was the one who grew to over twenty pounds on very little food and became a diabetic, and far too sweet and angelic for this place.

Twas not during my time, but the black cat with the crooked tail, grew into the black cat with the crooked back. The black cat who danced across the hot, hot stove of my mother's childhood.

This is what I was told about the hissy cat named Stitch: Once settled in the house, he will unlock the box containing the second-hand luck-of-the-Irish, will drive the clown car clear into town and back again, is the one who owns the chaos of the world. No wonder.

There was, there was, and yet there was not a long, slim calico by the name of Piccolo. She was sixteen and new. And then she was gone, too.

## Ode to the Sliver in My Left-Hand's Middle Finger

Oh, such a sliver
you are. So dark,
and fat and stuck
there. Your life was
eons long before you
finally decided to live
in the tender house
of my middle finger,
and are now lounging
on the thin hammock
of skin just below
the cuticle and—thankfully
not under—the nail.
You were born in
the forests, but came
to me disguised as
a partition of an
old wooden California case
that organizes letterpress type
to layout broadsides and
books to be printed.
So cultured you are!
Oh, dear sliver, how
thoughtful of you,
in bed for days
in my middle finger,
which, surprisingly, is not
even infected. Three cheers
for you on that!
There's a cat scratch,
too, beside you, from
a young tomcat I
once thought pretty nice—

four small lines, but
unlike you, they are
puffy and angry red
and hurt a bit.
Alas, another sliver has
stabbed into the tip
of my index finger.
This one lets me
know any time anything
touches it—it's a
jealous dog, and bites.
But you, oh, ancient
splinter, I didn't even
notice you were there.
When I finally did,
you were mistaken for
an errant pen stroke.
But you did not
disappear upon washing my
hands; did not abandon
me though you were
given a spit wash;
have stuck with me
through the thinnest skin
on my middle finger.
You're a fat, black
bird who sits lightly
there on my finger;
a check mark on
today's to-do list. "Yes,
yes, I'm here," you
say. And you are
still here. I can
see clearly that you
aren't planning to go

anywhere until I go
to work with needle
and tweezers and yank
you out.

## Last Year's Lost & Found

On a day so hot, our boredom sizzled and popped;
a day so sunny, our souls were blind by purity,
three brothers and I stood before our empty
elementary school, daring each other to go in there.
It was summertime, and the doors were locked.

The doors were also chained together
like prisoners. The lowest glass in the entry door
was already shattered, pieces glittering like jewels
on the black mat inside. Skinny little kids, we shoved
ourselves through the serrated window, across

the crystalline shards, and into the stuffy hallways
of our abandoned school. A dim glow shone through
the windows of the shut classroom doors, a kind
of secondhand light. The bell of white noise
clanged in our ears as we tip-toed down the hall.

We checked each classroom door. Locked. Tried
the restrooms. Open, woo hoo, but beyond dark, and
who knew who might be in there. We snuck past
the Principal's Office, and were delighted
to notice the Lost & Found bin still on the floor

filled to the brim and overflowing. This was the treasure
of the dropped, the abandoned, and the long forgotten.
And it was open for grabs: grubby winter coats, honey
gloves (paired and not paired), a new saddle shoe (black
and white, my favorite, but, oh man, just the one).

We weren't even to the bottom yet. We found
yo-yos, a baseball bat, peppermints, even, and then—
a small box filled with loot: bracelets, rings, necklaces

earrings—a booty of plastic, glass, and metal. A golden
bracelet dangled huge pearls, spiky shells, starfish.

That's the thing I grabbed as we heard footsteps echoing
off the far end of the hall. My brothers' fingers, too,
were suddenly full of plunder, and we ran quick and quiet
as rodents, like vermin, down the dark hall and out. The footsteps
rushing toward us became our own racing toward home.

## A Lesson Learned

In the old church,
on the hard, dark pews,
it grew hot and hotter
through the stained glass.

My little jacket was deep blue
with four buttons and two pockets.
One without a single hole. And oh,
glory hallelujah! Wads of gum
stuck under the pew, some stickier
than others. My fingers soon smelled
lusciously of peppermint, clove, and spearmint.

And then came the sin, of course.
Who could resist? That devil.
Little kids can do things like this.
The unraveling of innocence begins
simply enough. Chewing
other people's gum without remorse.
Savoring the flavors. Testing the suppleness
of the old and the used. Gaining
the understanding that, yes, it's true—
gum actually does keep its flavor
when put on the bedpost overnight.
Even someone else's gum.

## Learning to Dance

As I grew up I learned
that dancing is a sin,
flaunting the body like that.

I'm not sure what the crazy devilry
we did was called when the rhythm
of music was involved.

When we played records with the waltzes
from Strauss, for example, we'd end up
out of breath and dizzy, practically dying,

with all those whirling twirls in the living room.
Baby dervishes, graceless, but not disgraceful.
There was no stopping us.

## Bezoar for My Youth

I remember sitting at my spot
at the dinner table. Hours
would pass. I'd be the only one
left. On my plate,
the evening's vegetable:
canned spinach. A pseudo-food
with the taste and texture
of a dirt slurry, which I
couldn't stomach. Left at the table
with my plate cooling for five hours,
seven to midnight, a two-
tablespoon heap at the edge.
Once in a while, my head would nod,
or I'd be in a dream world even I
can't remember, and I'd be told
to sit up straight and eat. With the look
and possible taste of a wet homunculus,
I wouldn't eat a tine-full,
or even make a move for the fork.
Early on, when I took a stab
at eating just a bit, the sandy grit,
the saline of a dirty sea,
were followed by
a hearty retch. The length
of time spent staring at the withered
pile of blackened green
eased into me a new strength.
Even a kid like myself
can grow a resistance, a bezoar
against a poison, not
a cure, but a protection. Once
the successful act of stubbornness
was complete, there wasn't a chance
I'd accept a single mouthful.

Sitting there in the dark, as though
I was an old lady, I would eat only
what I wanted, leave the rest,
saying simply: Here I am. This is me.
The poison dispelled.

## Enunciation of the Minced Oath

When you are seven,
and you come into the house,
and you slam the door, and
say, "Darn it"
loud as you can,
you've done something risky.

Even when you're nine,
and you trip on the sole of your shoe
that's loose and flapping on the pavement,
and you say, "Goll!" loud enough
for the neighbors to hear, you know
you've done something really stupid.
But no one learns much on the first
transgression. An error must be repeated
and repeated until every facet is memorized.

Because, when you're seven,
those two little words can bring forth
the recurrent memory of the frothy taste
of an orange bar of Dial soap. So hideous
is this that, as an adult, you will
never purchase that brand.

But at seven, it's not just the soap,
and the froth, or the choking,
nor the retching, but the hand
of the mother who grips
your neck, and holds you
over the sink with the bar
of soap in her other hand,
and places it on your tongue,
and holds it there, patiently,
while you squirm and wiggle

like an insect, and she's scolding you,
loudly, about the blasphemer you are,
and the sinner, and the trespasser you are,
and her face is red, and her lips are tight.
You can see this is so even though
the water is pouring, and the faucet
is silver, and the sink is stained
and rusty at the drain, and the bubbles
are beautiful as they spiral around,
down, and out.

## The Scope

When I was a child,
under the hot summer sun,
I did not tan. My freckly skin believed
in burning—the bright red blister
and puff—under the joyous

gush of clouds. Was it you
who mentioned the discovery
that a magnifying glass can create
a small, fiery dot—
given the flare of the sun overhead—
and an unruly yearning to burn?
And why only half the story?
Even so, I was told, and then
I couldn't drop the curiosity
about the red and black ants who
bustled around under the sticker bushes.

I watched an ant
for half an hour, maybe more.
He wandered in a general direction
but digression was the rule, meeting
one ant, then another. He looked beneath
a rock, poked a dead grasshopper,
pulled at a stick.

But then a round, magnifying glass
appeared in my hand. Magic? Yes,
as pure as dandelion fluff.

And then it was I
who focused the bright pin-
point of light to shine
down upon the concrete,

wind its way across the gloss
of laurel leaf, and then grow small
and smaller on a pine needle,
before eagerly locating
the suddenly startled ant.

Did you understand what agony
looked like under such bright light?
The stark curl of it? The rounded hunch
of smoldering blame? Did you?
And what about the acrid aroma
of pain? The sizzle and smoke
in the true and beautiful curves
that wrestle with mortality. Now,
there's a race you can't win.
Tell me if you knew.

The ant, at least, had friends
who picked him up
and carried him away, actually
helped him to shake it off,
to come back into the world again.

Is this why you and I
show our fists to
each other, then—trying
to see a little better—come closer,
closer, then back away
till we are small as ants
with our microscopic outrage
against the universe,
against eternity,
against the puny white dot
of ourselves?

## The Phone Rang Just Before Breakfast

An awkward teen-aged girl answered.
The voice on the other end of the line
spoke quietly, reassuringly, suggesting
that the dog be put down.

*What? Must be a mistake*, the girl thinks.
*Wrong number? My dog is around here
somewhere. T-Bone? Hey, T-Bone!*
Though the dog didn't come running,
the girl didn't comprehend the words
she'd heard. Said she's call back later,
and wrote the veterinarian's number down.

The first understanding of anguish
comes like a sound, a low easy throb,
a heartbeat. Or it is like the mute-red light
some remember as seen through
the womb, as a little one edges
her way out. Later on, this dark-red glow
arrives first thing in the morning—
sunlight falling through the window
and across the bed—to the one who sleeps
causing a bright heat to roll across her face.

It turned out that T-Bone was hit by a car
in front of our house after tagging along
on a paper route with a brother. She
was the family dog then. After the accident,
she became my dog. I carried her
up the basement steps and out every day
for weeks, and back down again; fed her
the best canned dog food I could find, until
her bones mended enough. She became
the first "inside dog" our family ever had.

Have you ever noticed the heat sunlight
creates just above your closed eyelids
while you nap? Some days,
it's barely enough to notice.
Other days, the warmth coats
the entire body in a thin film of sweat,
which feels just like crying,
but without the sadness.

T-Bone lived another twelve years.
Her splintered pelvis healed.
She had a pin in her leg that kept her limping
and alive. Sometimes, I sleep with the sun
fierce on my eyelids, so I can remember
the warmth of childhood when we were
still whole and disaster-free.

## Wet Heads

My fifth-grade teacher, Mr. Yurina was a new,
exuberant teacher. He loved to read us stories after recess.
Just before the next recess, he gave us an ominous warning—
"There's a rainstorm outside," he said. "Do not
get your hair wet, or I will cut it off. Repeat:

Do not let your hair get wet out there!" Then he lined
us up and shoved us out to an overcrowded overhang
beside the school. The rain was thick as syrup
as must have been witnessed by Noah just before
the ark was pushed off for those forty days.

Us fifth graders could carry on just fine without the use
of the drenched swing, the monkey bars, or the toothless lab
named Lucky. "Sensational, isn't it," I thought, "how rain
can bounce and slide like marbles across blacktop?"
The diversion of shiny objects should be an omen of dread.

And then I heard my friend hollering for me
to "Come over here! Let's do something!" from the overhang
on the other side of our ell-shaped school. On that day,
it was a credible enough mirage that made it possible to slip
from one overhang to the other and remain reasonably dry.

"Okay!" I shouted, "Here I come," and ran like mad. When
the recess bell marked the end of time, I tore back across,
and headed for the door to the classroom. Inside again,
it's story time, and Mr. Yurina wants to read. "But first,"
he said, "I need to check for wet-heads. We know—don't we—

the wet head is dead." There are certain times when a shy person
can disappear. It's an easy trick—the soft focused eye is downcast
like shame, and she is gone. No eye contact means no one is there.

Mr. Yurina, scissors in one hand, begins to walk the aisles.
Each head he passes is palmed by the other.

"Dry," he says. "Dry...Dry...Damp." He hesitates,
and goes on. "Dry...Dry." Down the first aisle, up the second,
down the third. Then it's my turn for the touch. He taps my head.
"Wet!" he says, amazed, and stops. The classroom gasped.

Scissor blades sharpened themselves in the air.
"But I'm invisible," I think. "I'm not even here."
He pulls a hank of my hair up, puts scissors to scalp,
and I am scissored. I'd never heard a class laugh
as hard as goblins before that day, on and on,
an echoing nightmare. The classroom became a stage

with one spotlight glaring onto my neck. I tucked my head
into the crook of an arm like a bird who's trying to sleep.
And that is where I cried as quietly as an utterly mortified
and humiliated child could. How would I tell my parents?
How much did he cut off? Did he cut it right to the scalp?

How long will it take to grow back? I don't think I was able
to pull myself together before the bell rang to let us go home.
I walked by myself, and sulked all the way home.
When I got in the door, I showed my mom
the terrible after-recess hair cut. She looked carefully,

but didn't see any snip, or cut, or trim, or missing bit.
And then she started to laugh, grabbed a pair of scissors,
held them to my head, and to my shock, cut another
swipe of hair. She laughed and laughed.
"See?" she said. "Nothing," and showed me how scissors,

when set onto the skull and snipped, will make a noise
inside the head that sounds exactly like just fresh cut hair.

Later, that same rainy afternoon, I was sent to the corner for chasing after my four brothers, scissors in hand, asking, "Would you like a hair cut? Hahaha!"

## One Morning, and the Window

While on the phone with my sister,
I'm looking at a ladybug run
like mad across the windowsill.
Six tiny legs moving—machinery
on overdrive. She is burnt orange,
and has six spots, rivets dotting across
the middle of her shelled wings.

The window is smeared with dirt
on the outside, and grime on
my side. The ladybug passes
five dead flies, and two
of her species who've faded
to light tan. They may be dead,
but they look like they're
on vacation, lying under
a stark sun.

Beyond the window,
I see autumn's long yellow
grasses rustling in empty pastures.
On the other side of the third
barbed-wire line to the south,
there seems to be a new boulder
with a back-lit auburn glow. No...
two of them! Dark objects blurred
and shining in the distance.
They are shaped like cows,
or goats.

Still on the phone, I'm
pacing along the dark green floor,
giving energy a chance to escape.
Wood shows through the paint

from a history of pacing.
The ladybug, too, has begun
to run back, then stops
as if she slipped a cog.

The boulder nearest the fence
suddenly picks up its head,
flops its ears out, and
becomes a deer shining
in the brilliant sun.

Funny how my body plays tricks,
the eyes are magicians, the ears
jokers telling truth in puns,
and the brain has become
so stingy of late.

The ladybug
has now disappeared,
and the deer has put
her head down,
is a boulder again.

My sister has said goodbye
and hung up a while ago.
The phone is back in the cradle.

But more importantly,
the ladybug, now
dragging its half-moon up
the pane, has chosen
the vertical path. Good advice.
And the boulders
have moved further west,
like deer,
browsing.

## Without the Sun

Summertime, and the rain's still rattling down.
We were kids and this was our summer vacation.
We were supposed to be outside goofing off,
having some fun, but the rain taunted us for days.

We made a plan to head to the park beside the lake,
and go for a swim, rain or shine. We made
peanut butter and honey sandwiches, and
crammed them, with our swim suits and towels,

into brown paper bags, and started out. It poured
all the way there. By the time we hit the parking lot,
our bags had liquefied, and our lunches
were wrapped in our soaked-through towels.
We were shivering and bickering.

We dared each other to put on our suits.
We put on our suits.

We dared each other to run in the rain to the shore.
We ran in the rain to the shore.

We dared each other to step into the lake.
We stepped into the lake.

We were so easy.
We were startled

to find the water warm.
Summertime!

## The Homestead

Near Sappho, on the peninsula,
is a place quieter than you can count.
There's an old barn with short-tempered
chickens and sunny kittens. An easygoing cow
with big horns. Beside the house,
a nine-foot high fence surrounds
a profusion of vegetables in the garden.
The wire fence keeps the deer and elk out,
usually. A trail runs clear down
to Bear Creek off the Sol Duc River.
The water so cold it could freeze
your feet, even in summer,
stand there too long.

This is the place my Great Aunt Olga
homesteaded. She cooked for the hunters
of elk and deer, gave them a place to stay.
And then she'd laugh,
because the hundreds of elk
meandering around the pastures and hills
the day before hunting season began
would disappear entirely
for the next several weeks.
But she made a grand oyster stew.
That made a difference somehow.

## A Ride Through the Park

We are pedaling like freaks
through the deep woods of North Seattle
where small saw-blades
of salal scratch our legs,
and cedars reach out
to grab at our hair.
Little droplets in the alders
spit in our faces.

There's a rumor about a rapist
who lives in one of these trees.
We don't know which.
But he seeks the smallest
of the angelic children
who play at hiding in the woods,
and then they cease to exist.
We don't even know
what a rapist is, but the word
tastes like fear, and
we are hungry for it.

The chilled October air
does something to our bodies,
which feel red and threatened,
congealed with cold. The brakes
on our fat-tire bikes
protest and squeal. This
is not the adventure
of Sally and Dick.

When we were young, we toyed
with fear—our favorite sport.
Now that we're older,

now that we know better,
we wear our dread like a uniform.

## Instead of a Dog

When I was small, we had a chicken
named Midnight: a feisty, black bantam.
Her sister, Moonlight, was stolen
by a thieving dog under a hot sun

before their first summer was through.
If we could find them, Midnight gave us
tiny eggs with buttery orange yolks
good enough to fight over.

We entertained the bored neighborhood kids
with her chicken tricks. She'd swing
on anyone's leg who'd stick one out,
then expect to ride it like a swing, or else

peck at the legs she sat on.
Our chicken was tough enough
to fight with any shoelace put in front of her.
She'd "rip its eyes out," had a hunger for violence

which satisfied the fat bully of our block.
Midnight was dog-faithful, a malicious jouster,
a secret relative from the old world.
She followed us around like a disciple.

If you looked, careful, into her eye, you'd see
the descendant of a prehistoric bird of prey.
When we were lucky enough to get
ice cream, she'd rest on an arm—

like a trained hawk—to get her share.
We were so young, we didn't know the difference
between surprise and generosity
when her beak dove deep into the cone.

Our education in ethics came from
a chicken with her head on straight:
a little, black hen
with ice cream on her beak.

## History Lesson in Four Parts

### *Loose Photo*
We were created through spark
and bristle. The family history
on my father's side, less than a century long,
is fragmented as torn paper. Grandma
is a profile on a photo tossed into a drawer.
She's maybe twenty-six. Across
the top, a date is handwritten
under her name: "about 1913."

Her face is in shadow.
Light falls gently
on the back of her sturdy young neck.
A spot of honey has dropped onto the print.
A smear of dirt remains. The whiteness
of her dress fades out before
the photo's edge. The image shows only
one eye, which is thoughtful
and intelligent behind a long nose.
Her dark hair is twisted, then
pinned at the nape. Her downward glance
seems to contemplate escape. Yet her expression
is pleasant, approximates a smile. You can't tell
from the photo who she was, where she
came from, or where she might have gone.

### *The Buzz*
There's a rumor lying around
that Grandma left Grandpa once: a desperate,
forlorn act. This was simply not to be unraveled.
A little bee, or bird, buzzed into her ear,
and she flew off, just like that.
She came back, her fists jammed
in her pockets, because there was no place,

really, to go. Would she have returned
if she knew her life would be a balance
of cooking and arguments? Grandpa's smoke
painted all the rooms amber. She let him
drop her off at church on Sundays.

### The Handy Man from Somewhere
Grandpa couldn't say where
in the world his father came from.
Or wouldn't. There's no way
to know which. He worked from town
to town as a cowboy, a fry-cook,
a nurse, a nail-pounder, and just about
anything else. Odd jobs. One year,
his fingers were frostbitten
from rail-hopping, he said.

Our family's hands are large
and tough, know how
to grind and slog. They sting
like hell on cold days.

### Frameless
Grandma wove herself into a woman
who enjoys the dry toughness
of over-cooked meat, the pallor
of white gravy, and a mist of hope
to iron things out. A jar of fireweed
honey on her counter sugars
to gritty crystals. In her eighties,
Grandma's fine hand-written letters
wobble into scrawls and scraps.
She mentions how the holidays
have emptied. Too much work
to clean up after. No one to finish
up the chores. Too bad that granddaughter

won't come 'round this year, she says.
She wears lenses thick as magnifying glasses,
and an expression severe and awestruck.
She clings to our history in dull sepia tones.
The edges of her form threaten
to fade off the cracked paper
and fall to the floor.

### There Was a Time

Her elementary days were spent in a brick-fronted rambler in North City, Seattle.
	A skinny kid made a habit of threatening her on the way home from school. He lived one neighborhood to the north, so she and her first grade boyfriend plotted against him like a tiny gang out for their first revenge. Together, they followed him to taunt and throw stones at him. She struck him in the eye. When she saw him again weeks later, he wore an eye-patch and was very polite.

For a couple of years she worked summers on Orcas Island.
	She wasn't good enough to succeed as a maid: too slow, too inarticulate, too spaced. Instead, she became a waitress, dishwasher and cook at the Surfsider. A smirking co-worker let slip that her current boyfriend once was a patient at the local sanitarium: didn't say why, didn't say when. She listened endlessly to Cowgirl in the Sand, and understood her friend knew what it meant to lose a brother to suicide.
That summer, she learned the benefits of work hard.

All through high school, she prepped for college,
	but learned, too late, that girls from large families didn't go. Competition with unemployed, wealthy college students convinced her to teach herself, to quit wasting money. She passed some exams and became a school bus driver and summertime waitress. She scarcely wore dresses again. Those too-large, hand-me-down frills became part of her church and school past.

For a few years, she grew chickens in Seattle.
	Her desire to travel the world became a chicken coop full of Rhode Island reds, New Hampshires and one Muscovy duck. The dull colors of Pacific Northwest autumn became the color of dozens of eggs in a basket. One hand in the earth, she

married someone who loved the chemistry of weeding and cooking. Earthworms became important as a tractor. Though the Muscovy flew the coop, the marriage was haute cuisine.

She became old on a street named after mid-day.
      Each duration of time was divided by notable events: birthdays, special phone calls, the passing of so many aging pets. Then came the death of her husband, then her dad. Missing something or someone became routine. She discovered there's always time for the next thing, and became gravid with age.

## Morphine

> *In the morning, when the new*
> *angel of morphine arrived...*
> *we funneled it into her...*
> *killing her as fast as we could.*
> *—Ellen Bass, excerpt from "The End" (The Human Line)*

Sitting in the living room, passing time
with a video game, it was possible to try
to ignore the fact that, close by,
my father lay in a bed, dying.

Weeks before, he'd confessed
he wanted to experience death
without medication, and, since there
was little pain, we agreed—no morphine.

A few years prior, when my father
retired, he took up walking, biking
and horseback riding—exercise
for a long and healthy life.

Hospice is a wonderful thing
for the dying. The family gathers,
nurses give proper care, and honor
is splashed about like holy water.

Medicare allows just six months
for a patient to finish out his time.
Despite my father's negative request,
a morphine drip is installed,

a basic setup for the dying—and
a shunt to ensure a painless death.
A video game to divert attention.
A mother who rolls the father over.

A film of pneumonia coats the father's
lungs. He begins the marathon run.
He is in bed, but breathes as though
he's in the middle of a long-distance race.

The mother and the daughter stand pressed
on each side of the bed, doing all they can,
which cannot be enough. They hold his hands.
They fluff the pillows, gently. They don't look

at each other. They peer into his eyes.
(He looks scared.) They imagine they can
breathe for him. He is not in pain. The father
continues his run—the partaking of breath

is now his only duty, and he is falling behind.
The daughter calls the hospice office, and
is kindly directed to push the button
on the morphine drip. The daughter

presses the button like it is a miracle cure.
The father can't tell the daughter, one way
or the other, if he wants the morphine
or not. (Drip, drip, drip.) He is not in pain.

The father continues gasping for breath
like an out-of-shape athlete. He is determined
to finish the race respectably. The daughter
makes more frantic calls to the hospice office.

Always the same reply: give him another drop
(drip, drip) of morphine. But he is not in pain.
It becomes obvious morphine is not a cure.
The daughter pushes the button anyway.

One does whatever the professionals insist
will help. There is only The Drip. There is
nothing else to do. The morphine is administered
with fervor (drip, drip) until he's run for hours.

He's making for the finish line. He is not
in pain. His breathing decelerates like
slow-mo at the picture show. His inhalations
become a suspicion, then imperceptible,

and then he quits. He is done. In a few
more days, the father's six months would be up.
You did it, Dad, the daughter thinks. Finished
the race in time. You've won, haven't you?

## Grocery Shopping with Mom

It's the middle of the afternoon, mid-week.
My mother is an old lady standing on her porch,
wearing a sweatshirt with chickadees on it,
a white hat with a bill, green polyester pants,
and sensible black shoes with white anklets.
She is a nice elderly woman.

We're going grocery shopping today.
She's got a list in her hand. The bones
of her hands have bumps on them, and
her stomach is round. Entering the store,
my mother insists on pushing the cart.
It acts like a cane, helps her maneuver
the long, white aisles. She chooses
a dozen small cartons of flavored yogurt,
French bread and French-cut green beans.
The beans are for her dogs.

She takes two large bags of candy,
Reese's Pieces and Hershey's Kisses
off the shelf. Later, she'll give one bag
to me: a token of her appreciation.
It's okay. I like candy. The diabetic body
of my mother babies a sweet tooth.

She does not drive anymore.
Not since that early morning when,
on her way to the vet to get her
dogs washed—one pug and one mastiff—
she missed a curve, jumped a guardrail,
and wound up at the end of a dead end.
She couldn't say how she got there.
She had no idea who knocked over

the "Dead End" sign, who hit
the picnic table and the cement planters,
or let fly the rubbish from the cans at dawn
that garbage pick-up day. The car
was totaled. She and her dogs
only slightly joggled. A simple miracle.
Low blood sugar plays tricks
with the mind sometimes.

Mother gets a ride from a friend to church
every Sunday, even though the friend once
said "Crap." When Mom tells me this,
the taste of Dial soap fills my mouth
and I can see evil swirling down a drain.

Today, my mother smiles as she pulls
brownie mix and cookies from the grocery
shelf, and sets them in the bottom of the cart.
A box of ice cream drumsticks
finds its way into her shopping cart
when no one is looking. She lives alone.
When she gets back home, she'll decide
she shouldn't eat the drumsticks.
Says the grandkids don't like them, and
will give those to me, too. I'll
have no trouble enjoying them.

At the pharmacist's counter, she buys
a few hundred dollars worth of prescriptions.
Her insurance makes it possible for her
to afford to be diabetic and arthritic.
She also gets two gallons of milk,
two pounds of butter and a two pound brick
of yellow cheese. She buys the higher priced
groceries because she knows they taste better.

She has trouble finding the dried fruit.
Everybody does. When we locate it, a bag
of prunes and one of dates are dropped
into the cart. Plus a bag of marshmallows.
She's old enough to know better.
When we get old, she says,
we've earned the right to do things
just because we feel like it.

If we know the things we do
may cause us pain, let them fill us
with utter happiness each time we partake.
Make it worth the while.
Let the others cringe.
We're short-timers here.
Sometimes, guilt tastes better
than milk and honey.

## Dark Chocolate and Almonds

We'll be going to the grocery store
soon. Gotta get some more
of those dark chocolate-covered almonds
because they are good for you,

because they are candy
with dark chocolate,
and there's almonds inside them,

because you ate
so darned many of them
on your visit yesterday,

because Jim says you did,

because I like them for breakfast,
and for dinner,
and for lunch,

because I want more of them
in the house,

because maybe they really aren't
all that good for you,
because the FDA and other agencies
and scientists haven't yet
made up their minds
about dark chocolate and almonds,
good or bad,

because I know—when I look
into the little tin in which they are kept,
and there are only two left—

that Jim has eaten way more
than his share,
and so have I.

I just don't want
to run out.

## Morning World

My son's rat died this morning. I walk the trail
behind the house, and past the pond, to bury it
in the quiet woods, when I hear a hawk calling.
Two red-tails hover above the naked alders.

The foggy light of dawn shines through their
widespread tails, glowing red as stained glass.
Their beaks open, and clear cries write lines
in an ancient language across the air.

A glance at sharp talons makes me wonder
if they're interested in this chilled rodent cradled
in my palms, and I become nervous. But the pair dip
their wings, and disappear into the low-hanging clouds.

They reappear like angels above me as I dig the hole,
and line it with moss. When I drop the rat in, the shape
of its body curls to the bend of the earth. Fertile mulch
showers from the trowel while the hawks circle above.

Their cries trail behind them as holy as untranslatable
scripture. Not until the small grave is filled with dirt and
moldering leaves do the hawks disappear into the clouds again,
and I head to the house with an urge to wash, to be clean.

## Driving Down Sunset

It's winter. Everything is cold—the weather,
the car, my bones. The days turn dark too early.
We're in the car going down Sunset Drive. The light
ahead turns red. Traffic is backed up, moving slow.

The wipers plod across the windshield. We're waiting
for the light to change, when out pops a deer mouse
from under the hood near the wipers, which I turn off
directly. There she is on the hood, leaning on the windshield.

She looks at me with her large black eyes, nose wiggling,
before she darts quick into the warmth of the engine.
The light turns green. My throttle foot slowly bears down
on the pedal. I worry she'll die on the hot engine,

or in the fan, or on the windshield because
I might need to use the wipers soon.
Or maybe she'll try jumping into traffic. I drive
onward, and turn into the church parking lot on the corner.

I get out, look under the hood. No sign of a mouse
anywhere. I spend hours, it seems, convincing myself
she let herself out in the graveled lot, and didn't turn back
for a look. Maybe she'll make her new home in the church.

## A Detail

The first time I noticed
the geometric pattern
on a spider's back
as a sand painting,
my mouth
filled with grit.

Yesterday, my son
stood in the doorway.
Sunlight obliterated him.

My sister,
pregnant with her second child,
points into the sun.
She sees the future,
sees long, fragile legs
clawing an invisible web.

The spider is offensive and indifferent
twirling like she is
from a strand in the wind.
She broadcasts an illusion of success,
recreates the redundant strands of a masterpiece—
a trap for the hapless. She hangs there
confident in holding tightly
to hardly anything at all,
and she makes it work.

## Under Direwood

Under the stand
of trees, near the coop,
we bring a tablecloth,
five plates and a platterful
of peanut butter and jelly
petite fours, tiny sandwiches
to fit small hands. Under
the trees of Direwood
the large and ancient grandmother
giggles and dances before
plopping onto the ground.
She rests with her back against
a thin mountain ash.

The grandkids, one on each side of her,
pour lemonade, pass plates,
arrange teddy bears.

## Right Angles

During hot weather, horses
don't pant like dogs (or even cats).
The two mares just stand and swelter,
letting the flies have their way.
They turn their bodies to the best angle
for picking up the slightest breeze,
and drift off in noonday dreams.
They are like sailboats that way.

When I pull out the hose,
they come trotting over.
With the cold spray turned onto
her back, the ancient one turns slowly
in circles like a circus elephant,
determined to get every side wet,
every convex and concave curve of her.
When, finally, she cools down,
she wanders off to roll in the dust.

The other mare doesn't turn circles.
She stands there, meditating on the way
clear water sparkles in sunlight;
how it lands on her body,
falling like driven rain,
the drum of it beating; she considers
to the temperature of horse hair
lowering from steaming hot to ice cold.
It takes a while. She inclines her head
so that the hose forces water
into her mouth. She lets her lips
hang slack. Water spills out.

Eventually, she, too, folds herself
into a patch of bare dirt and rolls.

When the horses are coated
in mud, they stand and shake
off a storm. Downwinders
learn to squint in this beauty.

## The Weather of Night Horses

It's February. The cold has frozen the ground
to submission. The placid moon hovers above,
higher than a horse's eye. The fields, fence posts,

even the rusted barbed-wire, illuminated with silver.
This is a fine time to get out and feed the horses.
The stars are so brilliant the tall grasses bow down

to them, crackling with frost. It's a good night
for the barn owl to hunt winter's skinny rodents.
Not a breeze to distract from the silence.

The trees have settled into a temporary calm.
In the dim light, the horses are the specters who
carry the night's darkest shadows. I set their hay

in the secrecy of the dark field, and whistle for them.
At first, nothing. Then, they wander out from behind
a large tangle of blackberry vines nearby. The stamping

of the hooves moving over the icy ground
is muffled in the bone-cold air. Closer, and you can see
the clear weather of horses. They come near,

nickering and nudging each other, and raise their heads
to look at the moon. The air fills with the mist of their breathing.
The sound electrifies the silence.

Along their backs, the hair is tipped with ice.
The night horses lower their heads to the hay,
and music of contentment begins.

## There Are Horses in Heaven

This is a secret you mustn't repeat:
There are horses in heaven.

They have been there always.
Even while here, they are aware of there.

Have you noticed how the horse
sleeps upright and ready, and seems

to be elsewhere? There are horses
in heaven who feast upon the golden sheaves.

They come to earth on the darkest nights:
the flapping of wings hushed like the owls'.

They stay with us, as though held in a palm:
think of a roughened hand curled around the reins.

They sometimes grant us wishes. They
relieve us of labor and sorrow. The horse

was in heaven before Adam met Eve.
When these firsts were evicted from the garden,

a horse took them to another.
The horse lives in heaven

wherever she goes. This is
confidential and true.

## The Redolent Wings of Dawn

The broken raven crashed
through our rec room window.
It's presence heavy and silent.
We bent to listen, a hand
behind each ear. The sound
of a fingernail tapping a rhythm
into glass kept us interested.
The house abuzz like a planet.
Each tone twirling slow into a dirge.
The wind carried them
away like a diva.

The reddening light of sunset
filled the room. Your elbows
came to rest upon the counter. Steady.
Steady. Did the pots and plates spin
around the room? Or is that just
how I remember it? Our hands,
our empty hands, opened,
reached for the double boiler, the soup
bowl, the ladle, each other, anything
we could find, just to settle things down.
The clock was a casino of time.
The seconds moved sideways like a secret.
Some mornings are such weird sunsets.

Our off-kilter lives spin onward,
into the scraggly trees of dawn.
If every day were like this,
out the door and down the hill we'd go.
We'd leave this island in a flash.

But this is a rare goose of a day,
and the final moments

will be a treasured memory.
Black birds skirt the sky
and sink over the ledge of pines.
This may be the best day of our lives.
We'll labor over the details,
try to get them right, but the task

is useless. This day
isn't that day. If a sparrow
were to hop onto the windowsill,
and begin a new song,
we'd have heard it before. We wish
we could fly, but we have only the wind.

## Time with Cats

> *Time with cats is never wasted.*
> —Colette

Two cats on a bed.
One crossing in front of the other.
Big grey coon cats.

They give each other
a high five,
claws out, heads bowed.

The one cat crosses over
to the other side of the quilt.
It lays down. Yawns.

The other cat sits up.
Yawns.
You've seen all this

while buttoning your shirt.
Combing your hair.
You think of your mother.

Maybe you should call her.
It's been a while. But
you have to be sure to stop

at the post office, and then
get some hairball remedy. Maybe,
while picking up the mail

you could send a card to Mom,
or an entire letter, even.
The cats have fallen asleep.

One is upside down.
It begins to purr.
This is a day not wasted.

## On Breaking My Leg

"Break a leg!" you said to me
just before the poetry reading.
Unfortunately, I didn't break my leg.
I only tripped
on the word "lazuli" over and over,
until I lost my balance,

but, no, my leg did not break.
When I re-read the poem,
I just stood there
mispronouncing "lazuli"
over and over again,
still not falling,
still not breaking my leg,
wishing I would just break my leg
and get myself hauled out of there.

But today, I realized
that if I were just to think
of the phrase "last July,"
I'd be able to say "lazuli,"
over and over without a mistake.
And though my leg may still not break,
I would at least be pronouncing
"lazuli" flawlessly,
I hope.

## Though Strange, Though Enough

There was a time I kept my heart as stowaway,
below deck in a dark and musty brig. I met you anyway.

You say, "A mountain never climbs the climber," but halfway
there, the observant one sees it has taken you anyway.

Dust in the wind is last summer's insect swarm, a strange decay
that glows in the sunset. I believe in you, anyway.

A toast. Another. Another. And then let's make our getaway.
Drive like mad. The road twists around for you anyway.

Undone. This life is a tower of vertebrae,
stacked and strung, you standing in the way.

Poets? Edna St. Vincent Millay? Or even Hemingway.
Neither sea nor season holds love like yours in any way.

Oh, ye of little grace, ye who spills café au lait,
there's nothing more to do. I love you anyway.

## Biking Up the Driveway and Back

Jim walks the dog every morning and evening,
but rides his bike to the mailbox. He believes
in the mystery of the arrival of the daily mail.

It's not that the box is too far for a daily walk,
but that it's just far enough to make riding
a bicycle meaningful. On the way back,

he leans forward as he pedals while steering
one-handed. The other, filled with a flock
of envelopes pressed tight to his heart.

He once peeked into three mailboxes per day,
each one met with the eagerness
of unwrapping a birthday present.

He believes cracking open a mailbox is more satisfying
than a gourmet meal. Once, when the flag broke off,
he replaced it with a large serving spoon painted red.

## My Life

Your slippers are
paired

beside the dresser.
They're woolly inside

but old as my
horse. Duct tape holds

them together like
you've done

these past years
for my heart.

## Night Air

When moonless nights
wake me from sleep,
and I look up
to see the stars:
        The Big Dipper,
        Orion's Belt,
        The North Star,
then I am free
to breathe deep in the night.
To calm myself down
to my nameless soul.
It is then I hear the silences

echoed by the distance of the stars.
I stand alone thinking
of all who might know me,
and who knew me when.
Their faces gaze down into mine
and I ask them—
        Do you still remember?
        Can you feel what I feel,
        my grief, my love, my desire
or are you just another fragment
of a dream still tangled in my hair?

The stars gaze back, calm and quiet.
There is no answer, no message,
no hair rising on the nape of the neck.
So I am still free to breathe
deeply of the night air.

## View from the Upstairs Studio Window

Out the second story window of the studio,
facing east, is a row of large evergreens and the sky.

It's dark now, but the day
is just beginning to brighten.

There are sequoias on the left
who have grown more than thirty feet

since I first met them.
There is a scraggy willow

who shades the walkway, and
an emaciated mountain ash.

But this window focuses
on the sky. Thousands of swans

have flown across its span at night,
and owls, and in daytime, ravens and wrens.

From this window, each new viewing
carries something new: a bird,

a leaf, the color of the light. Right now,
the sky is changing from the infinity

of night to the clear skin of the new day—
two things that bind our planet together.

I can't imagine anything
more necessary than this.

## Cabin on Lummi Island

Divided in two parts like a tenant farmer's place,
the hallway between completes the shelter.
Entering this cabin, I think "Grandpa!"
because it smells of old snoose,
junk wine, and aging wood.

Sometimes mice, sometimes bats,
join us in the evening like whispers
in the corners. This place mocks
my history, which is why
I feel so at home here.

## As Wild Geese Gather

This gentle place—where cool, gray mist meets the hushed,
    rough-hewn fields—
carries the whistling wings of wood ducks rushing from the pond,
and the scraggling of the heron, as she, too, hurries home
to the damaged cedar over the brim of horizon.

This gentle place—where cool, gray mist meets the hushed,
    rough-hewn fields—
has always been home. Rabbits and deer are welcomed by black-
berry knolls, hanks of canary grass, and pink feral roses.

This is the place where I will lie down on the dampening
ground, to soak up the earth's sweet music in the afterlight.
This gentle place, where cooling gray greets the rough-hewn fields.

## Vehicle of the Muse

The daydream yesterday began
nicely enough— in a hammock
swinging in the wind. Followed
by a twisted journey of butterfly wings
along the row of raspberry vines,
emptied now of their fruit.
Then, ah, the scent of the horse
comes into view, and the soft nuzzle
of her nose. White clouds
silken against a depth of blue.

During the night, a barn owl,
under the dimness of the waning moon,
was caught by a barred owl
above the chicken coop roof.
A tangle ensued. Their wings
beat wildly in a silence completed
with talon and beak. The rooster
crowed with great certainty. This was
three in the morning. At dawn,
the coop is calmly covered in plumage,
white and tan, and a wing tip, too.
The feathers drift around the fence
like dreams. And it starts again,

this reverie, which is likely
to continue all day, this preoccupation
of the world. If there's a shimmer
in a bush, a velvet scent in the breeze,
a whisper from the ferns,
the muse arrives on her bicycle.
Just hop onto the handle bars.
She will take you almost anywhere.

## Why Horses

The horses aren't stomping at the gate
this evening, but I spread their hay anyway,

and whistle for them to let them know.
Faintly at first, they are running

from the back pasture—hooves powdering
across the hot ground under the late summer sun.

They are galloping close, circle around, snorting
and shoving. Nearby, the lead mare stops, jerks her head

high, and blows hard through the flare of her nostrils.
One eye fierce looking straight at me. I reach up, and

she let's me pat her warm cheek and neck, pull
at her mane. The dusting of sun blesses all it touches.

## Gratitude

As a poet, I have been lucky to know a large catharsis of poets as thoughtful and encouraging friends. They have each added to a journey in poetry I was at first reluctant to take. I want to thank Lana Ayers and her husband, Andy Ayers, for their generous support and kindnesses over the years. Lana is an incredible publisher. Many, many, many thanks to Nancy Canyon, as she is a friend who surpassed everything a person can wish a friend to ever be. Special thanks to Judy Kleinberg, Jeanne Yeasting, and Jennifer Bullis, whose longstanding poetry prompt workshops have only gotten better and better—we've been at it such a long time, but our poems continue to be surprising and full of excellence. Nancy Pagh, you are a treasure. My sisters, Karen Koenig and Carol Bianchi, who let me teach them a little about writing poetry, since they think exactly like poets do. David Scherrer, thank you for inviting me to ride those horses over there, and sharing the idea that being near a horse is a privilege. Thanks to my good friends Flicka and Moby, the kind, spirited, soulful horses who taught me intricate details about respect and honor. And best of all is the fine poet, my husband-partner, James Bertolino, who has taught me more about poetry and publishing poetry than I ever thought I'd want to know, and I am glad for every little bit he shares with me. Surprisingly, I am a poet. Who knew?

## About the Author

Anita K. Boyle works inside, and around, Egress Studio every day. She has a love of the natural world that has become the material of her poetry and art. She retired from freelancing as a graphic designer, and is now focusing on her poetry and art, gardening and beekeeping.

As a poet, Boyle writes at least one or two poems per month, sometimes more. As an artist, she makes paper, assemblages, artbooks, prints, and also draws in ink, paints in watercolor. The two things, poetry and art, complement each other, both containing aspects and opposites of the other.

Boyle becomes motivated to create poetry and art because, daily, the natural world acts like a wise professor, teaching through presentation, which is an old way of becoming informed about the strategies for living a decent life, answering questions about things from birth to death, as well as before and after those two defining moments. It is inspiring to learn a thing or two from a tree or a towhee, a bumblebee or a pond. Boyle is a pretty good student who makes lots of notes. The exams are in the poetry and the artworks she produces.

www.ingramcontent.com/pod-product-compliance
Lightning Source LLC
Chambersburg PA
CBHW031147020426
42333CB00013B/551